RESOURCES

FOR

EDUCATING ARTISTICALLY TALENTED STUDENTS

RESOURCES

for

*E*DUCATING

*A*RTISTICALLY

*T*ALENTED *S*TUDENTS

GILBERT A. CLARK
ENID D. ZIMMERMAN

SYRACUSE UNIVERSITY PRESS

91 90 89 88 87   6 5 4 3 2 1

Library of Congress Cataloging-in-Publication Data

Clark, Gilbert.
   Resources for educating artistically talented
students.

   Bibliography: p.
   1. Gifted children—Education—United States—
Art—Directories. 2. Art—Study and teaching—
United States. 3. Educational planning—
United States. 4. Gifted Children—Education—
United States—Art—Curricula—Handbooks,
manuals, etc. I. Zimmerman, Enid. II. Clark,
Gilbert. Educating artistically talented
students. III. Title.

LC993.265.C54 1987   371.95   86-23183
ISBN 0-8156-2401-8 (alk. paper)

*Dedicated to all the exciting young people who have attended the Indiana University Summer Arts Institute*

This oil painting was done by a fifteen-year-old student in Indiana University's College Credit For High School Students visual art class. This painting is one of a series of painting sketches stressing observation of a live model. Photo by G. Clark.

$\mathcal{C}$ONTENTS

	Preface	ix
1	**Policy and Programs for Educating Artistically Talented Students**	**3**
	State Guide: Arts for the Gifted and Talented	7
	State Guides: Visual and Performing Arts	7
	State Guides: Gifted and Talented	9
	State Handbooks: Resources for Gifted and Talented Education	10
	State Handbooks: Resources for Artistically Talented Students	11
	Local Handbooks: Resources for Gifted and Talented Education	12
	Representative Programs for Students Talented in the Visual Arts	15
	Conclusion	28
2	**Initiating a Program**	**29**
	Stationery	29
	Brochure	30
	Mailing Lists	31
	Letters to Teachers and Parents	32
	Application Packet	32
	Registration	34
	Employment Forms	35
	Evaluation Forms	35
	Conclusion	35
3	**Identification Procedures**	**37**
	Current Testing and Identification Practices	37
	Screening Procedures	40
	Conclusion	51
	Notes	52

4   Instructional Materials   **53**

Student-Directed Materials for Instructional Enrichment   54
Teacher-Directed Materials for Instructional Enrichment   70
Creating Teacher-Made Instructional Materials   94
Resource Source List of Art-Related Catalogs and Materials   96
Evaluating Instructional Materials   106
Conclusion   106

Appendixes   **109**

A: Sample Forms Used by the Indiana University Summer Arts Institute   111
B: Sample Testing Instruments and Student Test Responses   138
C: Instructional Materials Checklists   167
D: Address List of Resources   170

Bibliography   **175**

PREFACE

*T*HERE has been a recent renaissance in the field of art education about educating artistically talented students. In 1981, art educators Karen Carroll, Gilbert Clark, and Al Hurwitz coordinated an arts for the gifted and talented special interest group as part of the National Art Education Association (NAEA) convention held in Chicago. This was the first time in many years that such a group was granted an active part of an NAEA convention. Approximately twenty-five teachers and administrators of programs for students talented in the visual arts made presentations and more than 150 people attended an opening and closing session. Enthusiasm for programs for gifted and talented students in the arts was evident.

One of the major topics discussed was the need for sharing information and establishing a means by which interested persons could exchange ideas and knowledge. The next year, at the NAEA convention in New York, we coordinated the arts for gifted and talented students special interest group and were impressed by the growing concern among educators in this area of art education. David Baker, editor of *School Arts* magazine, contacted us after the 1981 NAEA convention about initiating a newsletter as a column about products, programs, and publications for artistically talented students. We were able to announce, at the 1982 NAEA conference, that a column in *School Arts*, The Gifted and Talented Times, would begin in the Fall of 1982.

While co-editing this column, we were in contact with state directors and administrators of gifted and talented programs in the arts, publishers of books and resources for gifted and talented students, and teachers and students in special programs for talented students in the visual arts. The success of the Gifted and Talented Times in *School Arts*, a special issue of *School Arts* devoted to educating artistically talented students in November 1983, and responses to these materials attest to the need for sharing information in this area.

In 1984 the book *Educating Artistically Talented Students*, which we co-authored, was published by Syracuse University Press. This book presented a historical and theoretical approach to examining past and present practices and programs for educating students who are talented in the visual arts. Some practical information was included in this book, although the main thrust was academic. Our experiences with the *School Arts* column convinced us of the need to write a resource book that would be a companion volume to *Educating Artistically Talented Students*. There hasn't been a resource compendium available for teachers and program coordinators who are responsible for educating artistically talented students as there has for educating intellectually gifted and talented students.

Resources for Educating Artistically Talented Students addresses this void and is intended to be used primarily by elementary classroom teachers and art instructors, junior and senior high school art teachers, college and university art educators, and administrators and teachers of programs for artistically talented students; it also may be of interest to parents, state directors of art and gifted and talented programs, and others concerned with educating artistically talented students.

Resources for Educating Artistically Talented Students is organized into four chapters: Chapter 1, "Policy and Programs for Educating Artistically Talented Students," begins with a review of state policies about gifted and talented education and reports and examines state guides and handbooks relative to educating artistically talented students. The need for, and implementation of, information sharing among the burgeoning visual and performing arts schools and programs across the country is then discussed. Descriptions of six types of representative programs that serve students talented in the visual arts are presented in order to facilitate information sharing among similar programs.

In Chapter 2, "Initiating A Program," many practical suggestions are offered to help program designers and administrators initiate new programs or reconsider organizational aspects of existing programs. Sample forms, found in Appendix A, are shown as examples of sequential steps and processes, based upon the authors' past experiences initiating and maintaining a summer institute for artistically talented students.

Chapter 3, "Identification Procedures," begins with a review of current testing and identification practices of arts programs and critiques both tests and other commonly used measures. In an extended discussion of screening procedures, a sequence of steps and devices are suggested to identify a specific population of artistically talented students. Common identification and screening procedures are described and analyzed. Sample forms, offered as examples, are found in Appendix A.

In Chapter 4, "Instructional Materials," criteria used to select instructional materials for review are outlined, followed by annotations that describe and critique numerous student-directed instructional materials. Similarly, teacher-directed instructional materials are described and analyzed. An extended resource source list of numerous commercial sources and available instructional materials also is offered. Instructions and examples for creating teacher-made materials and evaluating instructional materials for artistically talented students follows.

Appendix A contains sample forms from the Indiana University Summer Art Institute; Appendix B includes testing instruments, grading guides, and samples of students' test responses. Appendix C offers instructional materials checklists. Appendix D contains names and addresses of organizations available as resources for administrators and teachers, as well as journals, other periodicals, and books not previously reviewed.

We have not claimed to review all commercially available materials appropriate for educating artistically talented students. We have listed those with which we are familiar and which we have used. We do, however, solicit your help in locating additional resources that you or others have used and found suited for the education of students talented in art. We would appreciate your suggestions; please send a title, source address, and a brief description to:

Dr. Gilbert Clark, Dr. Enid Zimmerman
Department of Art Education
School of Education 002
Indiana University
Bloomington, IN 47405

Resources

for

Educating Artistically Talented Students

A faculty member of the Pro Arts Summer workshop at the Mass College of Art instructs a high school student about how to solve a painting problem. Pro Arts is one of a number of residential summer programs for visual arts students offered across the country. Photo by Donna Paul.

POLICY and PROGRAMS
for EDUCATING ARTISTICALLY
TALENTED STUDENTS

*A*TTENTION to education of gifted and talented children has its origins in the work of Binet and Simon (1905) in Paris, France, after the turn of the century. All historians of this movement agree that in the United States attention to gifted and talented students had its origins in the monumental work of Lewis Terman. His early research (1906) and life-time devotion to study of gifted and talented students created the foundation of all such efforts in the United States. As early as 1906, Terman was studying intellectual differences of young people and this led, ultimately, to his *Genetic Studies of Genius* (1925, 1926, 1930, 1947, 1959, 1968) which is still in progress. Terman's creation of the Stanford-Binet Intelligence Scale, based on the earlier work of Binet and Simon, was the foundation of his life-long inquiry. For this research, Terman defined giftedness as a single dimension: a score of 140 + on the Stanford-Binet Intelligence Scale.

Paul Witty (1951), a contemporary of Terman, questioned Terman's work on several dimensions. Witty believed that Terman's definition of giftedness was too narrow and that Terman failed to account for minority differences, sex differences, and the role of self determination. Witty made a major contribution to the ongoing study of giftedness in the United States by his insistence on a more broadly based definition. Witty (1951) defined a gifted or talented child as one who shows consistently remarkable performance in any worthwhile endeavor. This definition, however, has been questioned by Newland (1976) as too dependent upon demonstrated achievement and that worthwhile endeavor is debatable and invalid as a construct. Questions have been raised that still remain unresolved. In 1970, a congressional mandate added section 806, "provisions related to gifted and talented children," to the Elementary and Secondary Educational Amendments of 1969 (P.L. 91-230). This mandate directed the Commission of

Education to study the state of programs and to offer suggestions for attention to gifted and talented students.

In 1972, Sidney Marland, the U.S. Commissioner of Education, reported to Congress the results of a five-year study. In this report, the current definition of gifted and talented students was given:

> The term gifted and talented means children and, where applicable, youth, who are identified at the preschool, elementary or secondary school level as possessing demonstrated or potential abilities that give evidence of high performance responsibility in areas such as intellectual, creative, specific academic, or leadership ability, or in the performing and visual arts, and who by reason thereof, require services or activities not ordinarily provided by the school.

This report was especially effective in guiding congressional decisions; most of its eleven major recommendations became governmental policies or decisions. A national survey summarized in the Marland Report revealed that 57.5 percent of school administrators in the United States believed they had no gifted students in their schools. The same survey showed that even when students were identified as gifted, one third were given no special instruction; the remaining two thirds largely received only token assistance in their schools. Marland estimated that fewer than .04 percent of the nation's one and one-half to two and one-half million gifted children were receiving satisfactory services. Most of these were concentrated in ten states.

The year of the Marland Report, 1972, was a landmark in national attention to the educational needs of gifted and talented students. In this year, an office of Gifted and Talented was established in the United States Office of Education. The CEC/TAG/ERIC network was established by the Council for Exceptional Children through its own resources and partial federal funding. This network made it possible for those working in gifted and talented education to share program information and research findings on a national level. In the same year, Congress established the National/State Leadership Training Institute On the Gifted and Talented (N/S LTI) in Ventura, California. The N/S LTI was committed, in all fifty states, to leadership for gifted and talented education and providing training materials to be used in support of gifted and talented education programs. This agency continues to serve in this role to the present.

For the first time in the history of American education, in 1975, federal monies were made available to gifted and talented education through a special provision of the Special Projects Act of P.L. 93-803, Section 404. In 1978, the Gifted and Talented Children's Act (P.L. 94-561) was enacted and this act incorporated the expansive definition of giftedness used in the earlier Marland Report. Almost immediately, giftedness in psychomotor ability was deleted as a major concern. It was felt, throughout the country, that students gifted in psychomotor ability were already receiving special attention and that their needs were being met by the schools.

In practice, most programs for gifted students emphasize intellectual abilities and specific academic aptitude. Children with talent in the performing and visual arts, who may not score in the superior range on intelligence or achievement tests, are generally neglected in such local programs. If they can afford it, parents of such children invest in private instruction or specialized training provided by local tutors or private arts schools. This has been reported in the Bloom (1985) studies of superior persons in which he has noted a cycle of extra-school instruction as typical background for high-achieving young artists.

In 1979, Zettel claimed that twenty-eight states did include some statement about high performance in the visual or performing arts in their definition of gifted and talented students; this does not mean, however, that these states had programs for such students. The levels of state and federal support for artistically talented students has varied widely since implementation of the Gifted and Talented Childrens Act of 1978. At that time, the percentage of states that stipulated identification procedures for various categories of giftedness included:

76% Intellectual Ability
68% Specific Academic Aptitude
64% Creative and Productive Thinking
56% Talent in Visual and Performing Arts
52% Leadership Ability (Zettel 1979)

By the late 1970s and early 1980, however, Khatena (1982), Jackson (1979), and Zettel (1979) were reporting that though there were thirty-eight states with Gifted/Talented legislation, fewer than twenty-five of these were providing any funding to G/T educational programs.

Khatena noted, in 1982, that about one-third of the states funded statewide gifted programs, largely in the intellectual and academic areas, one third of the states expressed interest in and support for G/T education, and the remaining third had little or no involvement at the state level. Most of the states did, however, have local programs in selected communities.

In 1984, we wrote to the State Directors of Programs for the Gifted in each of the fifty states and the District of Columbia, requesting information about programs for talented students in the visual arts. In 1983–84, Bachtel-Nash (1984) completed an extensive survey that is reported in her *National Directory of Programs for K–12 Artistically Gifted and Talented Students*. From these sources, twelve years after the Marland Report was issued, we can report the following data about programs for students talented in the visual arts:

> Nine states either did not respond to either survey or did not report any programs.
>
> There were ten state-supported programs for such students, including eight Governor's Schools.
>
> Within all of the states, there were
>> 52 arts magnet schools supported by local or regional educational agencies.
>>
>> 64 summer programs.
>>
>> 98 local school district programs within the school year.
>>
>> 9 private programs, and
>>
>> 7 Saturday School programs.

As we look at the results of these surveys, it is interesting to note that although Khatena claimed that 33 percent of the states had statewide programs for gifted students, only 20 percent had programs for students talented in the visual arts. The overwhelming majority of programs for students talented in the visual arts remain locally supported. District-wide or college-based programs are not state supported, although they contribute to a number of programs for students talented in the visual arts.

Although the Marland Report was a national policy document, in essence, the multi-dimensional definition of giftedness found there merely allows local school districts to decide what gifts and talents they will serve. As can be seen, young people who are talented in the visual arts are poorly served throughout most of the United States.

In 1984, to find out more about the current status of state policy and programs for artistically talented students, we requested information about services for artistically talented students including programs at all levels, art magnet schools, and state publications. To gather this information we wrote to persons listed in the directory of the Council of State Directors of Programs for the Gifted published in July, 1984. This directory includes state directors from all fifty states and American Samoa, Guam, Puerto Rico, Trust Territories, and Virgin Islands. We received responses from approximately half the State Directors of Programs for the Gifted. Only four indicated that their state office directs its attention only to needs of academically and intellectually gifted students. All but nine state directors indicated that local educational agencies in their states offer programs for students who are talented in the arts.

Of all responses to our request for information, only one state, California, sent a guide that specifically addresses policy and programs for students talented in the arts. The following section will contain a review of this state guide along with others that include some aspect of educating artistically talented students, list state and local resources for gifted and talented education, and describe state and local supported schools and programs.

STATE GUIDE: ARTS FOR THE GIFTED AND TALENTED

Arts for the Gifted and Talented Grades One Through Six, 1981. California State
Department of Education, State Education Building, 721 Capitol Mall, Sacramento,
CA 95821

This publication has been made available from the California State Department of Education. In this publication, Bloom's (*et al.*) *Taxonomy of Educational Objectives: Cognitive* has been used to design and present sample lessons appropriate to
each of the six major classes in the taxonomy. The Bloom taxonomy has been advocated
as a gifted and talented education model for many years. This is one of the first instances
of its translation into an arts program for highly talented students in grades one
through six. In the first six pages, each taxonomy class is defined and lists of verbs
related to each class are given that are intended to elicit appropriate responses
from students.

In Chapter 2, sample lesson plans are offered for creative movement and dance,
music, creative dramatics, poetry, and visual arts. Visual arts lessons about self portraits, masks, pop art, and mythology and art are offered. As examples, these lessons
provide models for program planning that cover each of the hierarchical classes in the
Taxonomy of Educational Objectives: Cognitive.

The remaining two chapters also provide important contributions to gifted education in the arts. Chapter 3 offers interesting sample lessons for comprehensive or interdisciplinary arts programs. Some of these integrations deal with visual arts and
dance, music and architecture, and instrumental arts lessons for language arts, social
studies, mathematics, and science. Chapter 4 is a compilation of elements and vocabulary in each of the arts: dance, poetry, drama, music, and the visual arts. Comprehensive arts programs are often clouded by vocabulary disagreements. This chapter provides a basis for clarification of terms in the various art forms.

The provisions of Public Law 93-380, section 404, are the foundation for this
State Department of Education publication. Under the editorship of Ann Bachtel, a
team of California teachers and arts specialists have created a useful and realistic document for teachers of students who are talented in the arts. The lessons are complete
and carefully organized but are limited in scope and depth. They are suggestive of how
application of Bloom's taxonomy to the arts might be accomplished.

STATE GUIDES: VISUAL AND PERFORMING ARTS

The Visual Arts in Iowa Schools, 1984. State of Iowa Department of Public
Instruction. Grimes State Office Building, Des Moines, IA 50319.

This state department publication is a policy document regarding visual arts
education in the state of Iowa. It is divided into eight sections: rationale for art education, curriculum, program recommendations, exceptional children, community re-

sources, career opportunities, art education and technology, and evaluation. Appendices include a state art framework and lists of state arts organizations and museums and galleries.

The section about exceptional children includes information and services for gifted and talented and handicapped children. This section begins with a statement that is interesting in light of the responses to our request for information from state directors of programs for gifted and talented students: "Most gifted and talented programs in Iowa emphasize general intellectual ability almost to the exclusion of visual and performing arts ability. However, the *Iowa Code* is quite clear in including visual art, creativity and specific ability aptitude in the legal definition" (p. 63).

The section about gifted and talented students includes a definition, guidelines for educating intellectually gifted students in the visual arts, and procedures for identifying and educating visually gifted students. These procedures place emphasis upon broadening studio-based programs to include art history, art criticism, and aesthetics, as well as evaluation. The brief inclusion of provisions for students who are talented in the visual arts is encouraging and can serve as a model for other states that wish to include attention to artistically talented students in their state art guides.

Visual and Performing Arts Framework for California Public Schools: Kindergarten through Grade Twelve, 1982. California State Department of Education, P.O. Box 271, Sacramento, CA 95802

The California Visual and Performing Arts Framework was designed to provide guidance for curriculum designers in (1) planning arts courses that include instructional objectives, concepts, activities, resources, and evaluation strategies; (2) creating curricula that take into account interrelationships among the arts and interdisciplinary relationships with other content areas; and (3) evaluating instructional materials designed for study of the arts. The framework is divided into an introduction, seven chapters, and an appendix. The introduction sets forth the framework's philosophy. Commonalities in arts education are discussed in Chapter 1. Dance, drama and theater, music, and the visual arts are discussed in Chapters 2 through 5. Chapter 6 covers interdisciplinary education involving the arts. Chapter 7 deals with program development. The appendix contains criteria for evaluating instructional materials and selected references.

Included in Chapter 5, Visual Arts, as in chapters about the other arts, are selected visual arts terms; components, goals, and objectives for students; developmental level charts; program development; staff development; human resources; community resources; students with special needs; multicultural education; evaluating student progress; and equipment and materials. The section about students with special needs includes a brief discussion about gifted and talented students that is integrated with ideas found in other parts of this chapter. Concepts found in the visual arts chapter, as well as those found in other chapters, easily could be adapted to educating students talented in the visual arts by stressing components of aesthetic perception, creative expression, visual arts heritage, and aesthetic valuing as suggested in the framework.

STATE GUIDES: GIFTED AND TALENTED

The South Dakota Guide for Education of the Gifted, 1984. South Dakota State
Board of Education, The Section for Special Education, 700 North Illinois, Pierre, SD
57501

  This recent state guide for education of the gifted is recommended for use by
local school districts in South Dakota as a model for planning, implementing, and evaluating services and resources for gifted and talented students. The guide contains a
statement of definition; South Dakota's law relative to the education of gifted students;
a philosophy statement; statements of needs, goals, program implementation suggestions; program evaluation criteria; resources and materials; South Dakota's five-year
plan for education of the gifted; and appendices. The areas in which gifted and talented
students are considered capable of high performance include general intellectual ability,
specific academic apptitude, creative and productive thinking, and leadership ability.
Although the area of visual and performing arts is not included specifically, references
to the visual and performing arts appear throughout the guide. On a chart of instruments recommended for identification purposes, for example, the category visual and
performing arts is included along with the four other categories mentioned above. Some
of the testing instruments suggested, such as the Horn Art Apptitude Inventory and the
Meier Art Judgment Tests, are outmoded and their use for identification of talented visual arts students has been questioned (Clark and Zimmerman 1984). The forms in appendices are invaluable to anyone planning a gifted and talented program in any area.
These sample forms cover topics such as areas to consider in planning a gifted program,
needs assessment, community resource survey, management evaluation form, news release form, initial referral, parent permission for evaluation, student behavior checklist,
notice of placement, letter of parental rights, sample individual education programs
(IEPs), questionnaires for students and parents, program evaluation by students, parents, and teachers, and special education compliance. These forms are diverse, of a high
quality, practical for direct program application, and provide an invaluable resource for
program planners anywhere.

Criteria for Excellence: Gifted and Talented Program Guidelines, 1983. Language
and Learning Improvement Branch, Division of Instruction, Maryland State
Department of Education, 200 West Baltimore Street, Baltimore, MD 21201

  This booklet was designed to help Maryland educators make appropriate
modifications in their current programs to meet the needs of gifted and talented students in their schools. According to Maryland law, a gifted and talented student is defined as "an elementary or secondary student who is identified by professionally qualified individuals as having outstanding abilities in the area of: general intellectual
capabilities; specific academic aptitudes; or the creative, visual or performing arts."
Maryland law also states that "a gifted and talented child needs different services beyond those normally provided by the regular school programs in order to develop
his potential."

Six major program components are addressed and criteria are set forth that establish optimal practices for each component. These six components are: identification of students, instructional program, teacher selection, staff development, program management, and evaluation. The criteria used for each component are clear, concise, and complete. Persons establishing a gifted and talented program of any kind could use the criteria found in this booklet as a checklist to be confident that all important aspects are covered and that they are being sensitive to the needs of gifted and talented students in their programs.

STATE HANDBOOKS: RESOURCES FOR GIFTED
AND TALENTED EDUCATION

Gifted Guide, 1984. Division of Special Education, State House Station #23, Augusta, ME 04333

The purpose of this handbook is to provide a list of names, addresses, telephone numbers, professional positions, and description of interests and programs of persons living in Maine who are willing to share their expertise with gifted and talented students in all areas. The handbook is designed for use by administrators, teachers, teacher educators, others involved in in-service and pre-service programs in gifted and talented education, and interested parents and community organizations. This handbook represents a first effort toward establishing a gifted and talented network in Maine and can serve as a model for others who wish to start a similar network in other states or local school districts.

Talented and Gifted Programs in Oregon: 1983 Directory, 1983. Oregon Department of Education, 700 Pringle Parkway SE, Salem, OR 97310

This compilation of Talented and Gifted (TAG) Programs in Oregon was initiated for parents and school personnel who are interested in contacting and visiting programs for talented and gifted students. State, district, and locally funded programs are described in categories of contact persons, target populations, program emphasis, identification procedures, delivery of instruction, management, and evaluation. Not all programs, however, are described using all categories. The majority of the approximately 120 programs described are for intellectually and academically gifted students, although a number emphasize the visual and performing arts. This publication provides an outline of information that may be used for similar programs in other states for describing TAG programs as well as persons to contact who may direct programs for artistically talented students.

STATE HANDBOOKS: RESOURCES FOR ARTISTICALLY TALENTED STUDENTS

GATE Visual and Performing Arts Resource Book, 1984. Department of Education, Division of Special Education, Gifted and Talented Section, Territory of Guam, P.O. Box DE, Agana, Guam 96910

Students, parents, teachers, and administrators in Guam will find this resource book useful in locating books, periodicals, films, recordings, and human resources that are related to educating artistically talented students in the areas of visual arts, dance, music, and theater. Section I lists eighty-six arts periodicals subscribed to by various public, private, and military libraries on the island. In Section II, arts books are listed and categorized by shelf numbers found in the main library and its branches. Tape and record collections found in these same libraries are listed in Section III. Art and music books, available to teachers at the Guam Teaching Resource Center, are listed in Section IV. In Section V are listed art and music films found at the Teaching Resource Center accompanied by a brief annotation of the subject matter and appropriate age group for each film. In the final section, lists of resource people who are able to serve as tutors in a variety of areas in the visual and performing arts are identified. Relevant information such as name, address, teaching skills, student pre-requisites, student age requirement, fee, location of lessons, and other information is included. Cultural organizations, culture-related projects, and local businesses that carry arts supplies also can be found in this chapter.

This type of resource book is a most appropriate model for a local school district or a large city school system with arts resources that are relevant to educating artistically talented students. A publication such as this that lists the location of resources can stimulate the use of these resources and save time in finding them. The short annotations for films are valuable and it would be helpful for the periodicals, books, tapes, and records to be annotated similarly. The list of tutors is an excellent idea and a similar listing, appropriate to many communities throughout the states, could be easily initiated.

Gifted and Talented in Visual Arts, 1983. Office of General Education, State Superintendent of Education, State of South Carolina Department of Education, Columbia, SC 29201

Gifted and Talented in Visual Arts is a booklet of resources sponsored by the State Superintendent of South Carolina. The booklet is directed to art and gifted program coordinators, teachers of the gifted and talented in the visual arts, directors of instruction, and school administrators. Information in the booklet was compiled by Thomas Hatfield, State Art Consultant, and Anne Elam, Coordinator of Programs for the Gifted, based upon a national survey of art and gifted educational personnel at state and local levels. The purpose of the booklet is to provide a practical resource for those responsible for providing programs for gifted and talented students in the visual arts.

There are 120 pages of practical, ready-to-be-used resources. Program planners or coordinators are offered a historical background, an outline for program content, descriptions of administrative arrangements for gifted and talented students, and many sample forms for communications with parents, students, school personnel, and the general public. Following discussions of characteristics of artistically talented students, there are many pages of sample forms for identification of gifted and talented students in the visual arts, applications, procedures, and instruments, nomination forms, and final selection and screening forms. Methods for collecting program data and guidelines for program evaluation, including a sample evaluation checklist, also are included. School systems, addresses, and other sources are cited in the booklet, providing opportunities to contact administrators of other programs throughout the country.

Gifted and Talented in Visual Arts provides guidelines for program planners and coordinators and sample forms specific to artistically gifted and talented students that easily can be adapted to local situations. Although many forms are presented, they are not analyzed or critiqued. Some forms are more adequate than others and finding applicable forms for local purposes may result in many trial and error efforts.

LOCAL HANDBOOKS:
RESOURCES FOR GIFTED AND TALENTED EDUCATION

Secondary Advocates for the Gifted: A Journal for High School Teachers of the Gifted, 1983. Virginia Department of Education, Albermarle County Schools, Charlottesville, VA 22901

A competitive Block Grant from the Virginia Department of Education made it possible for selected high school teachers, counselors, supervisors, and administrators to take graduate courses in various areas related to the education of gifted students. The intent of the grant was to form a group of educators who would become advocates for gifted students in their high schools. Many of these educators participated in a regional conference, "Secondary Advocates for the Gifted," and a majority of summaries from presentations they made appear in this journal.

Contributions are divided into school-wide, interdisciplinary, and discipline categories. Although many of the topics are not specific to educating artistically talented students, there are a number of general topics, such as gifted girls and young women, mentor programs for the gifted, student-owned and -operated theater, and running a talented and gifted program, that are related to educating artistically talented students.

In many school districts, there are educators and other resource persons who could be persuaded to give presentations at a regional conference about their work with, or research about, students who are talented in the arts. These papers could be reproduced inexpensively and distributed in local school districts. Of course, state grants are helpful and could be used to defray typing, editing, and some conference expenses.

Gifted and Talented Program, Procedures For the Identification of Gifted and Talented Pupils, Seminar Program For Gifted/Talented Students, The History Of the San Diego Gifted Program, 1980. San Diego City Schools Education Center, Room 3126, 4100 Normal Street, San Diego, CA 92103

The San Diego City Schools have had a continuously operating program for gifted and talented students since 1949 when they began experimental classes for gifted pupils in grades four through twelve. Throughout its history, the program has provided leadership within California and nationally for improved education for gifted and talented students. Unique educational materials and resources have been created and earmarked for gifted and talented classes within the city schools. Cluster classes and seminar classes also are available throughout the school district.

Program leaders in all parts of the country may be interested in the numerous publications offered by the San Diego City Schools as sources for ideas and procedures. The four titles listed above are basic documents that define program philosophy, identification procedures, descriptions of special program adaptations, and a history of this school district's efforts toward serving the needs of gifted and talented students. More than a dozen additional publications are available. These publications include evaluation, using Guilford's structure-of-the-intellect model, learning through inquiry, and a site management guide.

There are no specific titles in these publications that address talent in the visual arts, although arts activities play an integral part in many aspects of San Diego's gifted and talented programs. Many topics listed in these publications can be used in conjunction with gifted and talented programs with a focus on the arts.

Establishing Communication Among Leaders of State and Local Programs

There obviously have been efforts at state and local levels to develop guides and handbooks to help persons interested in forming new programs and provide information needed by administrators and teachers who have programs already operating in their schools. The examples of guides and handbooks just described can serve as models and sources of information and organization for those interested in educating artistically talented students. We suggest that if resources appear useful and appropriate to the needs of specific programs, they should be requested and correspondence should be established with persons who have similar interests in other parts of the country.

Within the past ten years, there probably have been more programs designed specifically to serve the needs of artistically talented students than have ever existed in the past. Many of these new programs have been designed by people who are not aware of similar program efforts that have existed or are evolving in other parts of the country. Consequently, there are a large number of new programs for artistically talented students that share some similarities, although they also have many philosophical, structural, and curricular differences. In recognition of this, we wrote in 1984 that, "as the number of programs increase, it is apparent that an information sharing network

This oil painting, by a student in the William C. Enloe High School in Raleigh, North Carolina, demonstrates both individualistic interpretation and high technical ability. Enloe High School is one of a number of arts magnet schools in the United States that serve a county-wide area. Photo by Betty Clark-Pritchett.

among program personnel needs to be created. Such a network could provide needed information in support of program improvement and curriculum development at each site" (Clark and Zimmerman, p. 169).

Others recognized this need and, as a result, created the NETWORK For Performing and Visual Arts Schools that came into being in 1983. A conference held in October 1983, at New Haven, Connecticut, brought together representatives of fifty arts schools from the U.S. and Canada who met to form the Network For Performing and Visual Arts Schools. Its purposes are to: "provide a linking system of communication on matters of mutal concern: to establish a clearinghouse for information and a locus for like-minded schools; and to promote opportunities for specialized education of students in the arts" (Eddy 1985, p. 2).

The organization now publishes a newsletter, *Network News*, holds yearly conferences, and, among other activities, develops standards and guidelines for arts education, supports research and disseminates the results, and helps establish laisons with accrediting associations and other art organizations. There are now over 150 members in the Network and membership is offered in three categories: institutional, associate, or individual. Emphasis is upon institutional membership for arts schools and arts programs within larger school systems. Additional information about this organization can be obtained by writing to:

Network For Performing and Visual Arts Schools
35th and R Streets, N.W.
Washington, DC 20007

REPRESENTATIVE PROGRAMS
FOR STUDENTS TALENTED IN THE VISUAL ARTS

In order for networking among programs for artistically talented students to be successful, it is important to have access to information about where programs exist and what is being done in those programs. Bachtel-Nash (1984) describes approximately 235 programs in her arts program directory and the NETWORK organization lists approximately 150 schools as members. These include, however, both performing *and* visual arts schools; many performing arts schools or community centers do not include visual arts in their curricula. Our own correspondence, based upon preparation of our Gifted and Talented Times column in *School Arts* magazine, has led to contact with over one hundred school programs offered specifically for talented visual arts students. Interestingly, the degree of overlap among Bachtel-Nash's, the NETWORK, and our list is relatively small. The potential, therefore, for networking is continuously expanding and the need for information sharing continues to grow.

Information sharing among programs that have similar organizational structures seems most appropriate and useful. In order to facilitate such information sharing, we will describe, briefly, programs that offer descriptive brochures or other forms of program information into the following six categories and list some *representative examples:*

Non-residential arts schools, full academic year

Residential arts schools, full academic year

Extra-school, non-residential arts centers, full academic year

Within-school, non-residential arts programs, full or partial academic year

Residential arts schools, summer programs

Arts programs in museums and other community agencies, special time schedules

Non-residential Arts Schools, Full Academic Year

This category includes schools designated as arts schools, including arts magnet schools, that offer specialized programs for artistically talented students who reside anywhere within the sponsoring school district. They feature strong academic programs as well as intensive, pre-professional instruction in the visual arts. These are, most frequently, senior high schools; there are some junior high school level arts schools now being established.

Baltimore School For the Arts, 712 Cathedral Street, Baltimore, MD 21201

Baltimore School For the Arts is a public high school as well as a pre-professional institution for the arts. It offers programs for students from grades nine through twelve who demonstrate unusual aptitude in music, visual arts, dance, and theater. Students study basic skills classes before advancing to specialized areas of study.

Booker T. Washington High School, 2501 Flora Street, Dallas, TX 75201

The Arts Magnet School at Booker T. Washington is offered for students in grades nine through twelve in a cooperative program with the business and professional community of Dallas. The school offers major areas of study in performing arts, dance, music, theater, and visual arts in two- and three-dimensional media. Students are encouraged to work with artist-advisors in a variety of commercial studios, art schools, or galleries.

Duke Ellington School Of the Arts, 35th and R Streets, N.W.,
Washington, DC 20007

Duke Ellington School of the Arts offers pre-professional training as well as a high-level academic program for students in grades nine through twelve. The visual arts curriculum is designed to lead students through increasingly complex exercises in drawing, design, art history, two- and three-dimensional projects, and studio electives. Fourth year students can participate in apprenticeship and supervised independent study programs.

La Guardia High School, 645 St. Nicholas Avenue, New York, NY 10030

La Guardia High School Of the Arts, founded in 1984, combines in one institution the former Music and Art and Performing Arts High Schools. The school draws students from all over New York City and prepares them for further study at colleges, art schools, and specialized art colleges. Through a rigorous art and academic curriculum, visual art students attend basic to advanced art content, art history, and elective classes. The goal of the school is to offer a diversified, intensive fine arts education to create artistically literate citizens as well as artists.

The Magnet Art Program, 77 Louis Pasteur Avenue, Boston, MA 02115

The Magnet Art Program is a visual arts, secondary program at English High School in Boston, conducted in collaboration with the Art Education Department of the Massachusetts College of Art. The college provides a director, coordinators, and faculty, as well as some art facilities not available at English High School. Courses prepare students for employment after graduation or for advanced study in a college, university, or art school. An extensive program is offered of visiting artists, field trips, exhibitions by students and others, museum visits, apprenticeship opportunities for advanced students, and other enriching activities.

The School for Creative and Performing Arts, 1310 Sycamore Street, Cincinnati, OH 45210

The School for Creative and Performing Arts provides a broad, intercultural, general education, including college preparation and arts-related vocational programs for qualified students from all areas of Cincinnati and tuition students from surrounding suburbs. Students are encouraged to develop art skills, intellectual abilities, moral character, and a sense of community responsibility through academic, visual art, dance, drama, instrumental music, and vocal music classes. Early skill development classes in the visual arts lead to advanced courses and career development opportunities in a variety of areas.

Residential Arts Schools, Full Academic Year

This category includes privately supported boarding schools for the arts and state-supported arts schools. Their attendance is voluntary, though selective, and not limited by school district boundaries. They are characterized by rigorous academic and specialized arts curricula. Students generally must maintain strict standards of achievement in order to continue in the programs offered at these schools. Obviously, they require tuition and residential costs and involve living away from home; the costs are often subsidized by scholarships or state-provided funds.

Alabama School of Fine Arts, 820 North 18th Street, Birmingham, AL 35203

The Alabama School of Fine Arts offers talented students, grades seven through twelve, opportunities to study creative writing, dance, music, theater arts, or visual arts. The primary goal of the school is to train artists; however, the school also serves as a testing ground for students who will eventually become professionals in areas other than the arts. Visual art students take daily studio courses, a year of art history, and complete a senior thesis based on a particular medium they have chosen to study in depth.

Florida School Of the Arts, 5001 St. Johns Avenue, Palatka, FL 32077

The Florida School Of the Arts is called Flo Arts by its administration and students. Flo Arts was established to provide artistically talented students who are oriented to occupations in the visual and performing arts and academic and arts education appropriate to their talents. The school shares facilities with the St. Johns River Community College and educates both high school and college-age students. Funding for the school is provided by the State of Florida, The Friends of Flo Arts Association, corporate support, and grants and gifts from other sources. Students can specialize in the visual arts, dance, music, theater production and design, or drama.

The Interlochen Arts Academy,
Interlochen Center For the Arts, Interlochen, MI 49643

The Interlochen Arts Academy is a year-round, private, secondary, college-preparatory school that offers a full academic and diverse arts curriculum. Its students come from forty states and ten other countries. Major programs are offered in creative writing, dance, music, theater, theater design and production, and the visual arts. Visual arts classes are offered in seven media and students are taught by eminent artists. Students also are required to complete a comprehensive academic program.

North Carolina School of the Arts, Post Office Box 12189, Winston-Salem, NC 27117

The North Carolina School of the Arts is one of sixteen institutions of the University of North Carolina. The school's focus is to educate talented students in grades seven through twelve and undergraduate through graduate college levels for careers in the performing arts as well as providing a basic academic program. Although established primarily for students from the southern states, students attend from all areas in the United States. There are over two hundred high school students at the school who study dance, design and production, visual arts, drama, or music. The visual arts program includes instruction in drawing, graphics, color theory, two-dimensional design, sculpture, ceramics, photography, and art history. Third-year students have an opportunity to elect advanced studio or theatrical design and production classes.

Extra-School, Non-residential Arts Centers
Full or Partial Academic Year

Many communities offer programs for artistically talented students by providing an extra-school facility. These may be a school site, museum, community center, or other facility with a specialized staff that serves selected students during some part of their regular school schedule. Students take their academic and other classes in their regular district school and travel to the extra-school facility, as scheduled, for specialized arts classes.

Art Enrichment: The Archer M. Huntingon Art Gallery and the Austin Independent School District. Archer M. Huntington Art Gallery, 23rd and San Jacinto, Austin, TX 78712

Cooperation between the education office of the Archer M. Huntington Art Gallery, on the campus of the University of Texas, and the Austin Independent School District has led to formation of an Art Enrichment Program. This program provides gifted and talented elementary students, grades two through six, opportunities to visit the Gallery and participate in carefully guided learning experiences and in pre-visit and follow-up activities. The curricula used in the Art Enrichment Program are guided by Gallery resources and reflect concerns of the Austin school district. Up to eight Gallery visits are arranged that capitalize upon changing exhibits and visiting artists' schedules.

The Center for the Arts and Sciences, Ruben Daniels Lifelong Learning Center, 115 W. Genesee, Saginaw, MI 48602

The Center For the Arts and Sciences offers students in grades seven through twelve opportunities to gain extensive knowledge and experience in academic studies, visual arts, and performing arts. This secondary gifted and talented program is open to all students throughout Saginaw County; students spend half of each school day at the Center and the other half at their home schools. Each art student spends two hours in an area of interest and half an hour in a course designed to develop understanding about the role that arts play in society. The goal of the visual arts program is to have students develop technical skills and experience with a wide range of art media.

The Fine Arts Center, 1613 West Washington Road, Greenville, SC 29601

This central Fine Arts Center supplements regular high school basic art courses. Students take both academic and art classes at their home high schools and, for two periods a day, go to the Fine Arts Center. A third period is spent traveling. Arts classes are available in ceramics, metal design, printmaking, painting and drawing, music, dance, theater, cinematography, and television. All costs for materials, tools, and instruments are provided by the students' home school districts.

Milwaukee Art Museum Satellite Classes, Milwaukee Public Schools, P.O. Drawer 10K, Milwaukee, WI 53201

As one of many services offered in the Milwaukee Public Schools for artistically talented students, the Milwaukee Art Museum Satellite Class program has received much publicity. Selected students from throughout the city are scheduled into two-hour, one-semester classes conducted at the museum. The school district pays a full-time art teacher who teaches at the museum and uses the museum's collection as a resource. Local artists also participate as guest speakers or as hosts in their own studios. Students also visit other museums, such as the Chicago Art Institute and the Milwaukee School of the Arts, as well as downtown Milwaukee private studios and galleries.

Old Donation Center for the Gifted and Talented, 1008 Ferry Plantation Road, Virginia Beach, VA 23455

The Old Donation Center houses programs for talented students, in grades four through seven, in music, art, and other disciplines. Students can take two-dimensional art, photography, sculpture, and ceramics classes that are taught in six-week units of instruction in depth. At the conclusion of a unit, students move to a new unit taught by a different teacher. The program is interdisciplinary and art study is related to the art world outside the classroom.

Performing and Visual Arts Centers (PAVAC), Dade County Public Schools Talent Programs, 1410 NE Second Avenue, Miami, FL 33132

The PAVAC program is a colloborative effort of The Dade County Public Schools and Miami-Dade Community College. The program is designed to provide specialized afternoon classes in the performing and visual arts for talented students in grades ten through twelve. Participating students attend academic classes in their home schools during the morning and are bused to community college campuses during the afternoons. Regular, workshop, and master classes are offered in dance, theater and media, music, and the visual arts. These workshops focus upon theory and skills necessary to prepare students for entry into universities, conservatories, art institutes, or the professional arena. Students are required to demonstrate their commitment and achievement in regularly scheduled performances, concerts, and exhibitions.

Within-school, Non-residential Arts Programs,
Full Academic Year

Administrators in many school districts have created pull-out type programs in which gifted and talented arts students attend special classes during part of the school day that are offered within the schools they regularly attend. This arrangement is one of the easiest to organize, conduct, and administer. Students are not transported to other places nor do they have to deal with more than one school staff. The key to success in these programs is a highly trained, experienced teaching staff and support programs for artistically talented students in all parts of the school. The art school within-a-school offers opportunities for rigorous, specialized classes for talented students that would be inappropriate for general arts students.

Advanced Placement Studio Art, Art Department, New Trier Township High School, 385 Winnetka Avenue, Winnetka, IL 60093

Advanced Placement (AP) studio and art history classes are offered in many schools throughout the country. This national program allows advanced high school students to earn college credits while still in high school. New Trier Township High School, as part of its gifted and talented program, offers Advanced Placement courses in many subjects involving studio art. New Trier AP Studio Art courses require students to spend forty minutes a day in a class that stresses observational drawing, slide lectures, and problem-solving projects. They also must spend at least forty minutes a day in a different studio class with another art teacher. An Advanced Placement Festival, at the end of each year, features a comprehensive display of student portfolios.

Artistically Talented Classes, Jersey City Public Schools, 241 Erie Street, Jersey City, NJ 07502

Artistically Talented Classes (ATC) are offered in all thirty-three elementary schools, in Ferris High School For the Visual and Performing Arts, and in special Saturday classes in Jersey City Public Schools. Elementary classes are offered in primary and intermediate levels as a pull-out program. Basic design is taught at the lower elementary level and creative thinking and problem solving is taught at the upper elementary level. The Ferris High School for the Visual Arts is a magnet program that draws students from a city-wide area. Students are scheduled for a minimum of two periods of special art classes daily and take their academic classes with other Ferris High School students. Students begin by studying basic art concepts and later specialize in advanced art classes. A Saturday art program for gifted students, grades six through twelve, also is part of the ATC program.

The Artistically Talented Program, Irvington Public Schools, 1150 Springfield Avenue, Irvington, NJ 07111

Art, music, and foreign language for gifted and talented students are program areas in the Gifted/Talented Program in Irvington, New Jersey. The Artistically Talented Program is designed for students from grades four through nine, with special talent in art and music; it takes place at designated Irvington community schools. Students take regular academic classes and concentrate on art study during a block of time each day. Visiting artists and professional companies perform at the participating schools and students visit museums, galleries, and other art resources in the Irvington area.

Carus School Talented and Gifted (TAG) Program, Carus School District #29, 14412 Carus Road, Oregon City, OR 97405

Carus School District is a small, rural elementary district. It consists of a single kindergarten through six building that is twenty miles south of Portland, Oregon. Talented fine arts students are identified at all grades and offered five-day workshops with professional artists that last sixty to ninety minutes per day. Primary grade students may take one or two workshops and intermediate grade students may take up to five workshops a year. Students are expected to learn and develop specific technical skills and produce creative art products. The general goal of the program is based on awareness that art is important in a well-rounded education. Carus School District displays student art throughout the year and sponsors a Fine Arts Night in which programs and displays by performing and visual arts students are featured.

EACH Art, Whitehall City Schools, 625 South Yearling Road, Columbus, OH 43213

EACH (Enrichment and Acceleration for Children) is a program for gifted and talented students in the elementary and junior high schools of Whitehall City Schools, Columbus, Ohio. Academic, music, and art classes are offered in a pull-out program at all grade levels. EACH art classes for grades four, five, and six are held one day a week for half the school day. The junior high EACH program involves seventh- and eighth-grade students in special classes at one school. Program goals include development of technical skills, use of a variety of media, expansion of cultural and historical knowledge, and awareness of the visual arts in relation to the performing arts.

Enloe High School—Visual Arts Magnet Arts Program, Enloe High School, 128 Claredon Crescent, Raleigh, NC 27610

This Visual Arts Magnet Program draws students from throughout Wake County to the Enloe High School, not far from the State Capitol Building in Raleigh, North Carolina. The school serves a student population with a regular program and gifted and talented students who can major in government and law, mathematics, science, international studies, and the visual and performing arts. Talented visual arts students study a year-long Fundamentals In Art course as a prerequisite to Atelier courses that are in-depth, Advanced Placement courses with sophisticated content. The school also offers an annual study tour in Europe during Spring Break and frequent local trips to galleries, studios, and museums in the local area. An Arts Guild, organized similarly to band booster groups, helps support and build identification for the Visual Arts Magnet Program.

Gifted Visual Arts Program, Boone County Schools, 69 Avenue B, Madison, WV 25130

Boone County, West Virginia, has a Gifted Visual Arts Program in which students identified as talented in the visual arts, in grades two through twelve, are offered pull-out classes taught by a traveling art teacher. These classes meet for approximately 180 minutes per week. Eleventh- and twelfth-grade students are offered college credit for participation in specialized pull-out art classes. The program's objectives stress the importance of art classes in general education.

South Center For the Arts, Southwood Junior High School, 16301 SW 80th Avenue, Miami, FL 33157

Students at Southwood Junior High School who are enrolled in the South Center For the Arts take two hours of arts instruction daily in one of the specialized programs in art, drama, dance, or music, and four classes in the regular program of the Dade County Public Schools. Seventh-, eighth-, and ninth-grade students from more than twenty public and private schools of Dade County are enrolled in the arts program. Visual art students can study drawing, composition, painting, commercial art, fibers, sculpture, and ceramics. The South Center For the Arts provides students with opportunities to receive advanced arts training and develop their appreciation of the fine arts both as performers and viewers.

School Of the Arts At Monroe, Monroe High School, 494 Averill Avenue, Rochester, NY 14607

The School Of the Arts At Monroe is housed in its own building adjacent to Monroe High School in Rochester, New York. All non-art courses are taken in the high school and dance, music, theater, and visual arts classes for gifted and talented students are offered in the arts facility by a specialized staff of arts teachers and visiting artists. Classes are offered for students in grades seven through twelve. Students talented in the visual arts must select a major in the ninth grade, specialize in a minimum of ten credits prior to graduation, and prepare a portfolio and one-person show as graduation requirements.

Residential Arts Schools, Summer Programs

Perhaps the most common type of enrichment programs are residential arts programs offered during the summer months. They are available across the country and usually take place on college campuses. These programs are sponsored by colleges or universities or by state departments of education that support Governor's Schools and summer centers. Summer art programs often are intensive, immersion-type programs that attempt to meet the needs of artistically talented students during the entire day. Students enroll from throughout a state or region, irrespective of school district boundaries; some programs draw upon a national or international audience. A number of programs are specific to the arts, whereas others are part of a general gifted and talented summer program. Many programs emphasize, or are restricted to, specific media or technologies such as ceramics, video, or computer graphics. These programs often charge tuition and residency fees that are relatively expensive.

The Arkansas Governor's School, Arkansas State Department of Education,
Little Rock, AK 72201

The Arkansas Governor's School is a five-week summer program offered at
Hendrix College in Conway, Arkansas. It is supervised and administered by the Office
of Gifted/Talented Programs of the State Department of Education. The state funds tuition, room and board, and instructional materials for each student. Visual arts classes
focus upon contemporary social and scientific problems and emphasize art knowledge
as a basis for creating art. Computer graphics, laser holography, and videocinematog-
raphy are studied, as well as more conventional media.

The Boston University Summer Visual Arts Institute, Boston University Summer
Visual Arts Institute, 225 Bay State Road, Boston, MA 02215

The program at Boston University Summer Visual Arts Institute offers high
school students opportunities to choose several art courses that they pursue in depth
for six weeks. The Institute is located within a large urban University, in a historic
city, and students have access to artists' studios, art galleries, museums, and cultural
sites. Professionals who work at these art-related facilities also are available to
Institute students.

Brevard College School For Gifted Students In the Arts (BV/SGSA), Brevard College,
Division of Fine Arts, Brevard, NC 28712

In this two-week summer program for students in grades eight through twelve,
classes are provided in the visual arts, dance, creative writing, drama, and music. Visual arts classes include areas such as art appreciation, drawing, photography, ceramics,
design, painting, and sculpture. The classes are held at Brevard College, located in
a small town in the mountains of North Carolina. Small classes and a small teacher-
student ratio allow intensive work on individual and small group projects; college art
faculty and guest artists provide instruction.

The Governor's Institute on the Arts, Castleton State College, Castleton, VT 05735

Two junior high and two high school students are selected from each of fifty-
nine supervisory districts in Vermont to attend The Governor's Institute on the Arts.
Students pay a nominal fee and study with professional artists, on a state college campus, and have opportunities to select a major or minor in areas such as modern dance,
jazz, drawing, painting, sculpture, film, photography, poetry, music performance, acting, and directing. Interdisciplinary activities are encouraged. All students and staff
members belong to a choral group that meets daily. Each student is responsible for initiating an arts project in his or her home town during the Fall following the Institute.

IU Summer Arts Institute, Department of Art Education, School of Education 002,
Indiana University, Bloomington, IN 47405

The IU Summer Arts Institute offers a program for artistically talented students in grades seven through eleven from throughout Indiana and other states. Students elect a major class in drawing and painting and choose two elective classes in

areas such as modern dance, drama, musical theater, mime, photography, computer graphics, sculpture, printmaking, or narrative drawing. Students attend arts classes for six hours daily. Additional arts-oriented activities include museum and theater visits, concerts, guest speakers and performers, as well as open arts studios and practice labs.

Maryland Summer Centers For Gifted and Talented Students, Gifted/Talented Summer Centers, Maryland State Department of Education, 200 West Baltimore Street, Baltimore, MD 21201

A unique set of opportunities for gifted and talented students from grades four through twelve who attend Maryland schools is offered by the Maryland State Department of Education. Courses offered at ten different sites and types of institutions include aquatic studies, science, problem solving, leadership, space-science, mathematics and technology, natural history, economics and government internships, creative writing, and visual and performing arts. Talented visual arts students from grades seven, eight, and nine elect from several two-week course options in computer graphics, ceramics, printmaking, photography, sculpture, and drawing and painting. Arts courses are conducted at Goucher College, Maryland.

New York State Summer School of the Arts, Room 679 EBA, State Department of Education, Albany, NY 12234

Five hundred high school students with exceptional talent in the performing and creative arts study from four to six weeks with nationally prominent artists in the New York State Summer School of the Arts. Six separate schools are conducted in areas of choral studies, dance, media arts, orchestral studies, theater, and visual arts. The schools are designed to assist students in planning professional careers in the visual and performing arts. The School of Visual Arts, conducted jointly on the campus of the State University College at Fredonia and the nearby Chautauqua Institution, offers classes in sculpture, printmaking, screen printing, drawing, and painting. Visual arts students work in two of these areas of study. The School of Media Arts, conducted on the campus of the State University of New York at Buffalo, offers classes in film, video, sound, photography, and computer arts. Media arts students are involved directly in media production.

The Pennsylvania Governor's School For the Arts, Box 213, Lewisburg, PA 17837

Each summer approximately three hundred artistically talented high school students, including many handicapped students, attend the Pennsylvania Governor's School For the Arts on the campus of Bucknell University. Courses are available in creative writing, dance, music, photography, theater, and visual arts. Visual art students can select from ceramics, drawing, jewelry, painting, printmaking, sculpture, and weaving. Related arts seminars are offered to help students understand and appreciate all the arts and students are expected to select elective activities in an art field outside their major.

Pre-College Summer Foundation Program, Rhode Island School of Design, 2 College Street, Providence, RI 02903

The Pre-College Foundation Program is an intensive five-week introduction to the visual arts, designed to help high school juniors and seniors examine basic design problems and experience a wide variety of media. Rhode Island School of Design faculty and visiting professional artists teach the arts classes. Art study in depth is encouraged and students are expected to spend thirty hours a week in the art studios. Two hundred and fifty artistically talented students from the U.S., Canada, Europe, and Latin America attend this program each summer.

Precollege Visual Arts Workshop, Syracuse University, 117 College Place, Syracuse, NY 13244

Syracuse University's Precollege Visual Arts Workshop is designed for talented art students who are interested in pursuing a professional career in art. This Workshop is a six-week residential summer program in which high school juniors and seniors can earn six college credits in classes taught by SU faculty. In the mornings, students attend introductory studio classes in drawing and painting. Afternoon classes consist of a series of three, two-week studio workshops in sculpture, communication design, and art and photo processes. In addition to the workshops, there are guest lectures, field trips, and a final exhibition of student art work.

Pro-Arts Summer, Massachusetts College of Art, 621 Huntington Avenue, Boston, MA 02115

Pro-Arts Summer is a six-week program for artistically talented students in grades ten, eleven, and twelve. It is sponsored by a consortium of the Boston Conservatory, The Boston Architectural Center, Emerson College, Massachusetts College of Art, and the School of the Boston Museum of Fine Arts. The state's Board of Regents and the Massachusetts Council On the Arts also help fund the program. Students enroll in music, dance, architecture, theater, or visual arts classes during the day and enjoy evening programs including museum visits, theatrical performances, and concerts during evenings.

Shake Hands With Your Future, College of Education, Box 4560, Texas Tech University, Lubbock, TX 79409

Shake Hands With Your Future is a gifted and talented summer enrichment program sponsored by Texas Tech University. The program, divided into two-week sessions, is designed to meet the needs of gifted students ten to fifteen years old, by introducing topics that are not commonly found in the school curriculum. Each student is assigned three daily one and a half hour courses or "quests" in areas such as math, science, engineering, architecture, computer science, art, drama, music, creative writing, and philosophy.

SUMMERART, Department of Fine Arts, University of Northern Colorado, Greeley, CO 80639

SUMMERART consists of two one-week summer institutes for artistically talented students from grades seven through twelve that take place at the Great Lakes Art Camp, adjacent to Rocky Mountain National Park. The instructional day is divided into two three-hour sessions and students chose classes in one familiar art area and one new art area. Advanced students are allowed to work semi-independently and earn university credits.

Summer Enrichment Programs, The University of New Mexico, Albuquerque, NM 87131

The goals of the Summer Enrichment Programs are to promote the development of gifted classes throughout the Southwest. Classes are offered on the University of New Mexico campus and at the Tres Lagunas Resort in Northern New Mexico in areas of micro-computing, architecture, interrelated arts, photography, and mime and magic. Five one week sessions are offered for students in grades four through six and seven through nine.

Art Programs In Museums and Other Community Agencies
Special Time Schedules

A number of arts programs and other services for artistically talented students are sponsored by agencies other than schools. Some schools also offer services in addition to the regular gifted and talented arts program. Options can vary from a museum-based program to a privately-owned art gallery that features student work. More of these alternative resources need to be created across the country to expand opportunities for artistically talented students and create broader public awareness of the capabilities of such students. Information sharing networks need to include optional programs and other alternate opportunities for artistically talented students in their communities.

Art Mentorship Program, The Amana Public School, Middle Amana, IA 52307

The Amana Public School is a small, rural school with a high school enrollment of about eighty students. In order to expand art activities beyond the classroom, talented art students can qualify to work with a local, professional artist in his or her studio. A list of available mentors is developed through input from area and state arts councils and area colleges. An individual education plan (IEP) is developed by the student and project art coordinator. Each mentor session lasts a minimum of three hours and there are usually six to ten sessions. The time together may include gallery visits and art events. The coordinator critiques the student's art work at the end of the sessions.

The Gallery, Suffern Junior High School, Hemion Road, Suffern, NY 10901

The Gallery at Suffern Junior High School offers artistically talented students opportunities to exhibit their art work. Exhibitors are responsible for mounting and displaying their work, designing invitations and posters, news releases, and hosting their opening. The school's music department provides musical groups to play at openings and a student photographer documents all openings. The Gallery consists of two glass showcases in the school's front lobby. A faculty sponsor directs The Gallery that has successfully drawn parents, townspeople, and local reporters. The Gallery schedule is reported in a local newspaper on a regular basis and feature articles also have reported past student shows.

GATE Visual and Performing Arts Program, Division of Special Education, Department of Education, Territory of Guam, P.O. Box DE, Aganda, Guam 96910

The Gifted and Talented in the Visual and Performing Arts Program on Guam is part of the Gifted and Talented Education Program (GATE). All students from preschool through twelfth grade are eligible for nomination to the Visual and Performing Arts Program. This program includes study of painting, sculpture, pottery, photography, and ethnic crafts. The GATE Program provides some in-school experiences and a wide range of out-of-school arts activities such as Resource Room Activities, Saturday Arts Program, Kid's Eye on Guam TV Series, GATE Summer School, GATE Workshops in the Arts, and special competitions and exhibitions. A local non-profit corporation teaches students art management skills and how to sell their art work at various shops on Guam.

Project Art Band, Education Department, De Cordova Museum, Sandy Pond Road, Lincoln, MA 01773

Project Art Band is a cooperative program between the De Cordova Museum and four nearby school districts. Artistically talented students in grades seven, eight, and nine are offered a number of learning opportunities through Project Art Band. These include apprenticeships with local artists, weekly in-school classes, and field trips to numerous art institutions. Student apprentices work with an artist for ten, weekly, three-hour sessions. In-school classes meet once or twice a week and are taught by local teachers. All participants attend field trips to the De Cordova Museum as well as such places as The Boston Museum of Fine Arts, the Isabella Stewart Gardner Museum, and local galleries and arts-related businesses.

Rainbow Connection Art Gallery, 100 Hudson Street, New York, NY 10013

The Rainbow Connection Art Gallery in New York City is unique because the forty artists who exhibit their work in the gallery are all under the age of seventeen. A sponsorship program helps young artists who are unable to pay the nominal fee that defrays gallery expenses. Sponsors share in the gallery's sales commissions. The gallery is a commercial operation and it reinforces professional status of the young artists and allows the public to view their work in an art gallery. Art work exhibited in the gallery is reviewed in many newspapers and art journals.

The Teen-Artist-In-Residence Program, Albright-Knox Art Gallery, 1285 Elmwood Avenue, Buffalo, NY 14222

The Albright-Knox Art Gallery sponsors Advanced Placement studio classes; selected students from these classes, on the basis of excellence and sophistication of their work, may be chosen for the Teen-Artist-In-Residence Program (TAIR). This program is sponsored by the Albright-Knox Art Gallery with funding from the Metropolitan Life Insurance Company. TAIR participants teach studio art classes in high schools other than their own. They are responsible for planning their instruction, proposing and completing an art project during their residency, critiquing their students' projects, and writing an evaluation of their residency experiences.

CONCLUSION

Art educators throughout the country should strive to demonstrate their support for statewide mandates and funding for educational programs that conform to the Marland Report's inclusion of giftedness in the visual and performing arts. Policy in this important area of art education is generally lacking and, where it exists, usually is local and idiosyncratic. Once states support and fund education for students talented in the visual arts on a planned and purposeful schedule, art education within these states becomes a focus of attention. Information sharing and networking for support of policy, programs, and publicity can add greatly to resolving some problems currently faced by programs for artistically talented students. This ultimately leads to improved art education for all students by demonstrating superior performance levels and supporting the creation of worthwhile and innovative curricula. This, in turn, leads to greater public support for art in all the schools because art is then considered as viable and important as other school subjects. The policy question, then, is whether or not art educators and administrators want to effect change through support of improved art education programs for students talented in the visual arts and how they will bring about this change.

One of the unresolved policy questions about education of the gifted was asked by Gallagher in 1975: "Can we find a way to modify public policy, which is traditionally geared to reacting to major crises, so that it can pay some attention to the long-range but gradual erosion of intellectual resources represented by our inadequate educational planning for the gifted?" (p. 305). The same question, greatly magnified, can be asked in relation to the needs of students talented in the visual arts.

INITIATING a PROGRAM

$\mathcal{T}$HE tasks associated with initiating a new program can be overwhelming. We have been conducting the IU Summer Arts Institute for over six years and have developed a program calendar and many forms and mailings that help make administering this program both easy and efficient (see pp. 23–24 for a description of the IU Summer Arts Institute). The following discussion offers suggestions about how to initiate and administer a program for artistically talented students. It is based upon administration of the IU Summer Arts Institute, a residential summer program conducted on a university campus, but could be adapted to any other administrative arrangements. The most common type of school-based program for artistically talented students across the country is summer enrichment classes. Private, year-round classes are also popular but less commonly offered for visual arts or theater students than for music or dance students. Our program, used as an example, is based upon attracting students who elect a visual arts major in drawing and painting and choose from dance, theater, music, and visual arts elective classes.

STATIONERY

One important step, when it is decided to offer a program for artistically talented students, is to select a name for the program and have stationery created with the name as a letterhead. If the program is located within a school, school district, college or university, or other sponsoring agency, such stationery helps create an identification unique to the program that provides an identity and insures that all inquiries and other messages are directed to the program's office. Another means of achieving a unique identification is to design a logo, to be printed on stationery and used in brochures and other publications, that graphically represents the program's emphasis. If it is strictly a

This linoleum cut print was made from sketches of a plant in Indiana University's greenhouse by an eighth-grade student at the IU Summer Arts Institute. The decorative lines and patterns and dramatic use of large positive and negative shapes make this an exciting print. Photo by Indiana University AV Services.

visual arts, dance, theater, or music program, or an arts program, the logo should depict these aspects of the program. After five years of using an adult-designed logo, we conducted a logo design competition among the 1985 IU Summer Arts Institute participants. This resulted in a new design with the appeal of being created by a young person attending the program. Two logo designs, one created by a college art student and the other created by a participant are shown in Figure 1 (Appendix A).

BROCHURE

We have examined a large number of brochures for arts programs offered throughout the country. These vary, on the basis of program resources, from profusely illustrated with colored or black and white photographs on up to twenty-five pages printed on slick paper, to a single-page folder printed with one color, without illustrations, on inexpensive bond. Although cost and quality may vary, any program brochure must be prepared carefully. A program brochure will, most often, provide a first impression of a program to readers. It is important that the brochure be well-designed graphically and answer major questions readers may ask. The brochure, especially if its purpose is to attract participants, needs to provide all basic information about the program and name a specific office or individual to contact.

Our brochure has evolved over several years. The specific information we always provide includes the program title, dates, a sponsor list, program description, criteria for nomination, tuition, related course announcements for teachers, and a complete list of courses to be offered. The program title and logo should match those on program stationery. Program dates are especially important; they need to be announced early enough to allow for advance planning. This is true especially for summer or other programs that go beyond the regular school day. A sponsoring organization or organizations such as a school, art department, or special services offices should be listed as a courtesy and acknowledgement. The program description should be global and answer questions about the program's focus, philosophy, organization, and schedule. It also should identify the program director and other faculty and staff associated with the program. Criteria for nomination should be stated clearly and specifically and include the eligible age group and who may make nominations. The tuition announcement also should be specific and describe all services covered by the tuition such as room and board and supply costs. If an organization sponsors related teacher workshops or other teacher services, these also can be announced in the brochure. A list of specific course offerings with titles and brief descriptions will help possible participants decide whether the program meets their needs. A contact person or office should be identified as a source of further information. Many program brochures contain an application form to be returned directly to the program office.

Some programs advertise through distribution of a large poster that contains most of the information found in a brochure. Posters catch the attention of teachers, parents, and students if they are placed strategically and are visually exciting. Posters, however, unlike brochures, usually are not sent to individual teachers and prospective candidates to keep for closer study and decision making.

MAILING LISTS

After creating a brochure, it is important to distribute it selectively to insure contact with the desired student group for whom the program is intended. Within a school or school district, it is relatively easy to obtain lists of students who might be eligible for a specific program. Programs designed for larger audiences, such as elementary or secondary level students within a state, or public and private school students within specific age groups, necessitate different procedures than those used within a school or school district. Most state departments of education maintain lists of all public and private schools within their boundaries and make such lists available to directors of educational programs with no charge or for a nominal fee. Sometimes these lists are available as gummed labels addressed specifically to art teachers within specific schools. If it is possible, information should be mailed directly to teachers by name. Generalized mailing lists containing only school addresses are not effective; mailings often are not forwarded to specific teachers you may want to contact. Preprinted, gummed labels or an addressograph program that prints gummed labels are efficient resources for brochure mailing. Brochures may be designed to fit into envelopes or mailers or, if carefully considered, can be labelled and mailed as a folded packet, without necessitating envelopes; the latter is a less time-consuming method of preparing information for mailing and is less expensive.

LETTERS TO TEACHERS AND PARENTS

We have found, in relation to the IU Summer Arts Institute, that a letter to teachers, requesting nominations, generates more responses than a simple program announcement. We send our brochure throughout the state of Indiana, addressed to specific elementary, middle, junior high and secondary art teachers. We also enclose a letter, addressed to teachers, inviting them to nominate students by listing their names and home addresses on a prepared form. This letter announces the program, restates the nomination criteria, and provides spaces for student names and addresses. A deadline is announced for receipt of the nominations. It is important, for public relations and continued support, to remember to send a letter of appreciation to each teacher who responds. Upon receipt of nominations, we send a brochure and a letter to parents of each student nominated that specifies that the student has been nominated by his or her art teacher and inviting application to the program. At the bottom of the letter to parents, a mail-in form requesting an application is provided. A sample letter to teachers, thank-you letter to teachers, and letter to parents are shown in Figures 2a, 2b, 3 and 4.

Any program that has been operating for one or more years should have a record of past participants. All past participants should be mailed, directly, an invitation if they are still eligible to reapply. These invitations may result in reapplication by a past participant and also may lead to applications by siblings and friends of past participants. We have had up to 25 percent of past participants reapply and participate in each year's IU Summer Arts Institute.

APPLICATION PACKET

All requests for application to the program are responded to by forwarding an application packet. Each packet includes much of the information reported in the brochure such as title, dates, sponsors, generalized program discussion, and list of courses.

More specific information is given about scheduling of morning and afternoon classes, recreation activities, and evening events.

The packet also includes information about specific aspects of residing in a campus dormitory, identifying a central contact office, tuition, and application deadline. Three pages of application forms are included. These are printed on colored papers for easy identification and referred to as yellow, green, and blue forms. The yellow form is to be completed by parents or guardians and requests information about the applicant, his or her family, and the applicant's past history of involvement with arts-related activities. The blue form is to be filled in by applicants and requests personal background information, selection of a major interest, and a rank order selection of specific elective courses described on the form. Final course offerings and related teaching staff are selected only after application packets with student elective choices are submitted. The elective course offerings are therefore based upon student interest and desire. The green form restates the criteria for nomination and is filled in by a principal, counselor, and art specialist or other teacher. They are asked to describe the applicant's major interests and strengths. These three forms are to be returned to IU with a $50.00 deposit, by a specified deadline. A copy of the IU Summer Arts Institute application packet is included as Figure 5a–5d.

Parents and applicants are notified after selection or rejection of applicants on the basis of their qualifications, fitness to the stated criteria, and to achieve balanced enrollment of sex, age, and grade groupings. A specified date of notification, two weeks after the application deadline, is stipulated in the application packet. A letter to parents welcomes their child to the program and stipulates a deadline for balance of payment that is approximately three weeks prior to the beginning of the program. Applicants receive a notification letter, with the parents' letter, that announces their selection for the program and invites them to "make new friends and enjoy the many arts activities" that will be made available to them. Sample parent and applicant letters of acceptance are included as Figures 6a and 6b and a rejection letter is included as Figure 7.

Acceptance letters are accompanied by a Program Information Packet. This packet outlines specific information about registration and residence hall requirements. Recommendations about clothing, spending money, visitation policies, and religious services also are included. Program procedures for residential and non-residential participants are included, such as when to arrive, where to unload baggage, how to register and receive a dorm key, and a schedule of events for the last day of the program. A number of forms, to be turned in at registration, also are enclosed; these include an Authorization For Medical Treatment Form (Figure 8), a signed Rules of Conduct Form (Figure 9), Clothing Inventory (Figure 10), and a release form for participation in research and use of photographs in future publicity or publications about the program (Figure 11). Two of these forms are required legally in order to protect the program staff and administration. These are the Authorization For Medical Treatment and the Research/Photography Release Form. The Rules of Conduct and Clothing Inventory insure that students come to the program knowing what is expected of them and leave the program, hopefully, with all the clothing they brought.

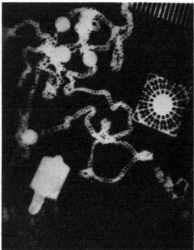

This photogram was made by placing various objects on sheet film and exposing it to light. A seventh-grade student, without photography experience, carefully arranged this composition at the IU Summer Arts Institute. Photo by Loret Falkner.

REGISTRATION

Registration can be a harrowing experience unless activities are carefully organized and monitored. A key to survival on a hot, summer day is to provide lemonade and enough cups and napkins for parents, participants, and registration staff. Registration should be sequenced into specific steps or stages with assigned responsibilities. These might include: (1) dispensing identification badges and meal tickets, collecting unpaid fees and handing out receipts; (2) collecting required forms such as Rules of Conduct, Clothing Inventory, and Permission/Release forms; (3) collecting Authorization For Medical Treatment forms and prescription medicines to be dispensed by the program's medical staff; and (4) handing out a Program Schedule, including a daily schedule, class assignments, room assignments, and a list of all participants names and addresses. At the final step, room keys should be assigned and key deposits should be collected if required. One person should be assigned as a trouble-shooter or problem-solver to work out, if necessary, program changes such as room assignments and class schedules. All participants' spending money should be collected during registration and released through a specific person in order to insure equitable spending and withholding during the program. Persons responsible for collecting forms should have a complete roster of participants and extra copies of forms; it is important that all forms for every participant be collected.

EMPLOYMENT FORMS

All faculty and staff associated with a program need to understand their responsibilities before a program begins. This can be accomplished by supplying each teacher and staff member with a program contract and job description. Each program contract should specify the amount to be paid and record required information such as a current address and telephone number, Social Security number, and signature of the employee (See Figure 12). A job description for teachers, counselors, and other staff members should be distributed that specifically describes duties and responsibilities (see Figures 13a and 13b). It is most important to hold workshops for faculty and counselors before and during a program. These workshops can be used to help coordinate activities, disseminate strategies for teaching and working with artistically talented students, and to improve teaching and counseling skills and techniques.

EVALUATION FORMS

As a program draws to an end, evaluation forms should be distributed and collected from students, teachers, counselors, and other staff members. Analyses of responses on such forms help evaluate the program and, therefore, help guide program adaptations each year (see Figures 14a–14c). In addition, other evaluation methods should include naturalistic methodologies such as interviews with participants and staff members, observations, and photographic records of activities. These evaluation methods supply in depth information about a program that cannot be gained readily from forms and checklists. Evaluation data should be kept on file from year to year to be used as a basis, with other program materials, for program changes, report writing, and program publicity.

After a relatively brief period, about two to three weeks, parents should be sent an evaluation form on which they are asked to report their child's and their own reactions and critique of the program. A self-addressed, post-paid envelope enclosed with this parent evaluation form and an introductory letter explaining the importance of evaluation feedback should result in a high percentage of responses. A parent evaluation form should include both open-ended questions that solicit unguided responses and suggestions for future programs as well as specific questions about the program. A sample Parent Evaluation Form is shown in Figure 14d.

CONCLUSION

Getting a new program started can be difficult and at times frustrating. Strategies and organization often have to be changed as needs arise and these changes cannot always be anticipated. We have shared some of our program's organization, structure, sequence of student, teacher, and staff responsibilities; forms to facilitate program activities; and hints about small services that make a big difference.

Each program for artistically talented students will have different philosophies, goals, objectives, and organization. Any suggestions offered here should be restructured to meet the needs of specific programs. It is important for administrators of a program to establish a calendar of events that should take place before a program begins. The more a program's needs can be anticipated and provided for in advance, the more smoothly the program will run. Of course, nothing is as valuable as experience. Be prepared to make many mistakes the first time around and record them so that they won't occur a second time. Soon you will become an expert with an efficiently running program and should be willing to share your expertise with others. Be open and continue to make constructive changes from year to year even when everything seems to be going well.

3

IDENTIFICATION PROCEDURES

W E attended a small group meeting at a local high school for parents of students who might be eligible to attend a newly formed gifted and talented English class. The criteria for entrance into this class, described as stressing great works of literature and creative writing, were that students should have high grades in their previous English classes, be nominated by their present English teacher, and have scores in the ninety-ninth percentile on the Iowa Test of Basic Skills, PSAT, or other standardized measures. We were upset and thought of the many students who would fall through the net and potentially be lost to this enrichment program if these were the sole criteria used. Most astonishing was the fact that samples of student writing or interviews were not being considered for entrance into the program. The more traditional identification procedures would encourage acceptance of students who were academically superior, good test takers, and conformist because these are the students teachers would be most likely to nominate. We thought how often similar procedures have been used to identify students for programs for artistically talented students.

CURRENT TESTING AND IDENTIFICATION PRACTICES

Current problems of identification, for any kind of gifted and talented program, frequently are examined in relationship to the practice of testing; testing is used in a very broad sense to include many forms of identification procedures. One way to examine current identification practices is to categorize them as the use of (1) standardized tests, (2) informal instruments, and (3) non-test methods. *Standardized tests* are defined as ones "in which the procedure, apparatus, and scoring have been fixed so that precisely the same test can be given at different times and places" (Cronbach 1960,

A criterion often recommended for admission to programs for artistically talented students is the degree of a student's interest, desire, and task commitment. This Alabama School of the Fine Arts student demonstrates concentration and complete involvement in his painting. Photo courtesy of Alabama School of the Fine Arts.

p. 22). Standardized tests include such instruments as the Stanford-Binet Intelligence Scale, IOWA Tests of Basic Skills, and the Seashore Measures of Musical Talents. Such tests also are standardized as a procedure with age and grade norms in order to expand their utility and applicability. *Informal instruments* are instruments that fail to control procedures, apparatus, and scoring so that their results, at different times and places, are idiosyncratic. Informal instruments include teacher-made, class-specific quizzes, performance checklists, and locally developed or single-use instruments of all kinds. *Non-test methods* are non-standardized procedures, such as self-nomination, degree of interest or desire, or past academic history, used to identify and select students for an educational program.

Although there are many current school, school district, and community programs designed to serve the specific needs of artistically talented students, there has been no consensus about recommended identification procedures or instruments for such programs. No current publication offers standardized, specific guidelines for the identification of artistically talented students that has been prepared by art educators or other arts professionals. In contrast, many psychologists or educators have written about academic or intellectual giftedness and have recommended specific instruments and procedures for identification (Guilford 1973; Khatena 1982). Some recent publications, in response to the six categories of giftedness outlined in the Marland Report (1972) and used by the United States Office of Education (USOE) have presented various standardized identification practices relative to each category, including the visual and performing arts. These sources are clearly reliant upon testing as an identification procedure, although standardized tests usually recommended have been shown, by others, to have problems and inadequacies for the identification of artistically talented students.

Creativity and Standardized Art Tests

Authors of major standardized creativity tests differ in their approaches to measurement. Some, such as Guilford, use tasks that measure specific, distinct behaviors that relate to divergent thinking. Others, such as Torrance, measure creativity as the result of complex tasks that require simultaneous application of many abilities. Both types of tasks, however, measure fluency, flexibility, originality, and elaboration as demonstration of creativity. Although some people have claimed that visual and performing arts giftedness is closely associated with creativity, others have raised questions about the use of creativity tests for the identification of artistically talented students. Recently, numbers of researchers have questioned whether creativity tests measure skills that students use in art tasks. As a result, students who score high on creativity tests may not, necessarily, be artistically gifted or talented (Lazarus 1981).

Current Identification Procedures

The Graves (1978), Horn (1953), Knauber (1932, 1935) and Meier (1963) standardized art tests have been evaluated by a number of reviewers. Many questions have been raised about their possible contribution or applicability to the problem of identification or selection of students for placement in programs for artistically talented students as well as other aspects of art education research.

If standardized tests are not recommended, what procedures should be used? It is most important that a combination of procedures be used as the most effective method of identifying gifted and talented students. A combination of procedures should include diverse sources of information that corroborate the desired characteristics from different points of view. What are the actual practices of identification and selection currently used in programs for artistically gifted students? We have recently surveyed selection procedures used in over fifty programs for artistically talented students offered in schools, school districts, community museums, and state or national programs (Clark and Zimmerman 1984). The following selection procedures are the most commonly used and are reported in order of their popularity: (1) self nomination, (2) portfolio review, (3) classroom teacher nomination, (4) interview, (5) creativity test, (6) informal art test, (7) art teacher nomination, (8) achievement test scores, (9) structured nominations, (10) peer nomination, and (11) parent nomination.

Actual practices of programs for artistically talented students throughout the country suggest that self nomination and review of a portfolio, judged by local criteria, are the most frequently used procedures. Most programs for artistically talented students, however, use a combination of at least three identification procedures for selection of students. Nominations of various kinds accounted for one-half the total number of procedures used in all programs. Not one of these programs used any of the standardized art tests available from commercial sources.

Schools considering implementation of a program for artistically talented students need to make decisions about program size, character, purposes, and available funding *before* identification decisions should be made. Identification procedures should then be designed that will screen and lead to selection of the number and specific character of students desired for a program. Current program procedures for identification of gifted and talented students typically admit from five to fifteen percent of local school populations. Decisions about program size obviously dictate that identification procedures be used that will achieve the desired population. Identification procedures should also be used to screen students as most appropriate to the types of classes offered. Criteria for entrance into a computer graphics program should differ from entrance requirements for a drawing and painting program. The critical prerequisite skills, abilities, and experience, therefore, would differ to some extent for different kinds of programs. The age group to be served, types of instruction to be offered, and goals of the program should guide decisions about the kinds of students to be identified.

SCREENING PROCEDURES

If school personnel are initiating a new program for artistically talented students, they may decide to be less rigorous about entrance criteria than if they had a long-established, well funded program to which many more students would apply than there were places available. Choosing appropriate screening procedures for identifying artistically talented students should be considered as a means of achieving a decreasing applicant pool. A first come-first served criterion would be least selective, followed by nonstructured nominations, structured nominations, achievement test scores, grades in art courses and other academic records, and informal art instruments. Portfolio reviews, auditions, interviews, and observations would be most selective and most costly to administer (see Figure 15, Appendix B).

Nonstructured Nominations

Nonstructured nominations simply ask nominators to recommend a prospective student. Various persons, such as self, peers, teachers, parents, counselors, and others can provide valuable insights about students through this procedure but the value of such nominations depends solely upon the information and insights nominators choose to include. Nominator bias, as well as lack of stated criteria, often results in either too little needed information or too much inappropriate information.

When students are asked to tell why they desire to enter a program, without specific guidelines to follow, they will generally provide valuable information about their interests, backgrounds, and goals. Student desire and interest is probably the most salient indicator for identification of artistically talented students. Persistent interest in the visual arts and a persistance of expressive effort are critical characteristics for the selection of participants.

As part of an application packet submitted to the IU Summer Arts Institute, a summer residential program for artistically talented junior and senior high school students, the applicants answer the question, "Briefly describe your previous art experiences and tell why you would like to attend the IU Summer Arts Institute." Answers vary considerably in both length and content but often supply useful information. The following excerpts typify the kinds of responses received. They indicate varying art backgrounds and experience, but all demonstrate a desire and interest to study the visual arts. The first statement indicates a rich background in art, well established goals, and obviously was written by a child who had traveled and was advantaged. The second statement shows a desire to study art, though it is based on more limited, localized, and diverse experiences. The student who wrote the third statement has a sense of humor, a strong interest in a specific time in the past, and is well-read. The fourth statement is short, direct, and demonstrates an intense involvement in making art.

Statement 1: "I enjoy all forms of creative arts, art history, art, and archeology. A recent tour of Egypt has sparked an interest in ancient art, including restoration and preservation of such art forms. Since drawing and painting are basic to all art, I want to continue my development in these areas. Through photography I hope to improve composition and collect ideas for future paintings. I enjoy creative writing and could combine this interest with illustrations in the Epics and Sagas class. Please see the yellow form for a resumé of my previous activities in the arts." This form included a list of accomplishments such as: twelve Scholastic awards, a County Art Association Award, first place in the state Symphony in Color Young People's art contest, artist for the junior high newspaper and yearbook, designer for her elementary school yearbook and tee-shirt logo, creator of the cover for a County Humane Society brochure, private instruction in watercolor and oil, and exposure to art history through tours of art museums throughout the world (Ninth grade student).

Statement 2: "I love music and art! I have been in the University Children's Choir for two years and I've been involved in our school choir for two years. I like acting. I also like to make things out of clay. I love any kind of camera class—movie cameras, cameras that they use at the library, and just regular cameras that are used at home. I took a camera workshop and I've been working with cameras at the public library for about two years" (Seventh grade student).

Statement 3: "I like drawing very much and I often doodle during breaks at school. I have drawn pictures ever since I remember because I like the imagination I can put into my drawings because there is no limit to the possibilities. I do not do much painting on paper, but I love to paint miniatures. Most of my miniatures are Dungeons and Dragons since historical ones are hard to find. I would like to learn to sculpt, but I have never done much beyond clay pots and play dough creations. I have taken a class in Basic Calligraphy because runes and gothic-type alphabets are interesting to me. I was inspired in writing alphabets by our German teacher, history, and books I read when I had a German class. I would like a good drawing class and a good sculpture class since I have "toyed" with the thought of being a designer for a company that makes miniature figures. I also like writing of all kinds except cursive" (Eighth grade student).

Statement 4: "I have been interested in art from day one. I have taken as many drawing classes as possible. I have drawn all my life. I love to do art" (Eighth grade student).

Such statements, along with other information provided on the application forms, provide insights about the applicants and help place them in appropriate classes. Such diverse responses are difficult to compare, and structured nominations in which all respondants provide similar answers are important to receive along with open-ended responses. They control the information reported and allow comparison of responses on different applications.

Structured Nominations

Structured nomination forms provide more useful information than open nominations because they require that the same information is reported for every applicant and can be tailored to the purposes and goals of a program. The stated criteria for selection of applicants are translated into questions on structured nomination forms and every applicant can be evaluated individually as well as compared to other applicants on each item response. Structured nominations can be solicited from prospective students and from parents, peers, classroom teachers, and art teachers.

Programs, purposes, and goals should guide preparation of structured nomination forms to insure efficient and effective identification of appropriate students. One of the most commonly available structured nomination forms is a behavior check list that consists of prepared lists of behaviors indicative of gifted and talented abilities in specific categories. Users are asked to check the observation of, or to rate, the presence of specific behaviors. When rating is added, each behavior is judged for its frequency or strength as well as its presence. No art products or auditions are required. A few nationally available behavior checklists for art specific behaviors (Renzulli, et al. (n.d.); Khatena 1981) do exist and have been used by programs in several parts of the country.

There is still need for greater development of behavior checklists for visual arts programs to improve their standardization, clarity of terms, and their ease of use. Behavior checklists used by parents, teachers, peers, or others requires training so that the terms used are understood in the same way. Checklists that use several measures of differentiation provide results that are superior to simple checklists of characteristics.

Self and peer nominations are valuable for identifying artistically talented students. Students usually know their own skills as well as the strengths of other students in their classes and in extra-curricular and out-of-school activities. Artistically talented students are often very self-critical and able to assess their own desires, interests, skills, and abilities more perceptively than others. Nevertheless, nomination efficiency requires the preparation of peer- and self-nomination forms that are appropriate to program goals, clear and easy to use, and easily assessed by program staff.

Self nomination

Students are often good judges of their own interests and abilities. A self nomination in the form of a self-interest inventory can identify pertinent hobbies and interests of students that relate to goals of the program. Self-interest inventories can yield data about students' beliefs about self, general beliefs, goals, and values related to artistic achievement.

Figures 16 and 17 are two examples of self-nomination forms. Figure 16 is a simple check list and, as such, provides a limited amount of information and does not differentiate between students with average and high abilities who may have similiar experiences in their backgrounds. Figure 17 uses open-ended, but structured questions in which applicants can describe qualitative aspects of their experiences.

Peer nomination

Although many gifted and talented students often conceal their abilities from teachers and other adults in their schools, they are generally well-known to their peers. Peers know one another in out-of-school and other nonacademic contexts where their abilities often are openly shared. Peer nomination, therefore, may identify individuals who may be overlooked by school staff members. Peer nominations may require students to list other students whom they would describe as matching specific criteria (see Figure 18) or nominate specific students and rate their art-related behaviors on a scale of frequency (see Figure 19).

Asking students to list other students they believe are talented simply elicits a list of names as possible candidates. It does not differentiate between the relative abilities of the candidates, though it is effective as a preliminary selection procedure. More specific information is gathered by asking students to nominate specific individuals and rate the frequency of their art-related behaviors. The frequency rating provides information that can be used to guide more efficient and effective selection procedures. By asking for additional comments, as in Figure 19, information may be obtained about peer perceptions that also may help guide selection procedures. The examples in Figures 18 and 19 are for intermediate or middle school grades. Others would need to be adapted for primary or secondary school usage.

Parent nomination

Parents often, but not always, know their children better than teachers and administrators because they are able to see their children in multiple social situations outside school and at home. Of course, parents of gifted and talented students often are biased and may under- or overemphasize their children's accomplishments for various reasons. Recognizing this potential for bias precludes using parent nominations exclusively; parents can supply types of information that school personnel or peers may not be aware of or report. Parent nominations may take the form of an open invitation to write a letter or a structured form to be filled out. A simple checklist or yes-no answer form should be avoided. A parent nomination packet should include a form on which parents rate the frequency of art-related behaviors and generally describe their child's interests and activities that relate to potential success in a selective school program. Figure 20 represents a sample form that can be adapted to specific program needs.

Teacher nomination

Evidence presented by researchers has demonstrated, over and over again, that an open-ended invitation for teachers to nominate gifted students has yielded very poor results. Research demonstrates that teacher judgment alone catches only about 20 percent of gifted or talented students (Boston and Orloff 1980). It is possible to greatly improve the effectiveness of teachers' nominations by providing structured nomination forms that state specific criteria and by in-service education about nomination criteria and methods prior to the nomination process. Some programs for artistically talented students are using these recommended practices to improve teacher nominations.

Figures 21 and 22 represent two forms of nomination that can be used by teachers and others associated with a school program. Figure 21, an Art Behavior Checklist, requires rating the frequency of observed behaviors and adds a feature, weighted results, that helps guide selection processes. The frequencies are weighted; the check marks in each column are added and multiplied by the weight value assigned to each column to yield a weighted total for each column. The column totals are then combined to yield a single score as a numeric value that represents the nominee's behaviors and behavior frequencies. The value of this practice is that it yields a single numeric score for each student and these can be used to compare the entire pool of nominees. On Figure 21, the nominator is asked to supply additional comments and these also

Visual narrative drawing has been used as an identification task and in the IU Summer Arts Institute it is the basis of an elective class. This narrative drawing, by a ninth-grade student, is one page of a six-page story. This student's abilities are evidenced by the drawing quality, placement of figures in frames, and highly imaginative tale. Photo by Indiana University AV Services.

should be used to guide selection decisions. Figure 22, a Visual Arts Assessment Form, combines a checklist and subjective questions. These help form an overall profile describing important work habits, art knowledge, and motivation levels, elaborated by open-ended questions, that can be used to guide selection decisions.

We suggest that various combinations of checklists and subjective questions are superior to either practice used in isolation. Both non-structured and structured sources of information are important because they yield very different information. It often happens that an insight obtained through non-structured or subjective reports is vitally important to those decision makers who select students to participate in a new program.

Group IQ and achievement tests and academic records

The use of standardized group IQ and achievement tests are recommended by many people and the usual criteria is for scores that are two or more years above grade level. This recommendation is based upon research that has shown that students who display unusual abilities in music and art are usually intellectually superior and are frequently achieving above grade in their other school subjects.

Group IQ and achievement tests are good for screening purposes but should not be used exclusively for final identification. These kinds of tests are easy to administer and lower in cost than individual tests, although individual tests yield more reliable scores. Content of group IQ and achievement tests, however, is not always suitable for identifying gifted and talented students in the arts. These kinds of tests fail to identify from a quarter to a half of gifted and talented students in the visual and performing arts (Pegnato and Birch 1959; Boston and Orloff 1980). Creative and divergent responses are penalized, rather than rewarded, on these kinds of standardized tests, as they frequently are in school classrooms.

It is true, however, that the great majority of students who qualify for special art classes are students with superior grades and superior test scores on IQ or standardized achievement tests. This relationship has been noted for well over seventy-five years and is found again and again in the writings of those who have analyzed artistically talented students (Clark and Zimmerman 1984). We frequently receive test score reports with applicant's papers submitted for the IU Summer Arts Institute; these often include 90th to 99th percentile standardized achievement test scores. A characteristic of Summer Arts Institute students, often surprising to new faculty or other program staff, is the intellectual, physical, and emotional maturity they demonstrate while in the program.

Informal art instruments

Many local visual and performing arts programs administer group drawing tests, ask students to submit slides of their art work, or require that students send video or audio tapes of a performance as identification procedures, especially at the junior and senior high school levels. Visual arts students often are asked to submit from ten to twenty slides of their work for consideration. Often, students are not given specific criteria about how their art work will be judged. Locally created criteria frequently are used to make selection decisions, although they often are stated in very open and ill-defined terms such as "creative" or "original," "uses color," or "uses form." These criteria are checked on prepared forms as checklists, without qualifiers. Such criteria and procedures fail to guide judgments, are often very subjective, and are based upon personal reactions that lack sufficient information to be justified or defended. More needs to be done in the development of instruments that can be used in all parts of the country, accompanied by objective criteria systems, including materials for the training of judges.

The work-sample technique offers an alternative to subjective measures and provides answers to most criticisms that have been cited. In work-sample procedures, a common assignment or group of assignments, is given to all applicants and evaluation criteria are established to grade results of the assignment *before* results are obtained. The technique has a long history in visual arts programs, going back to the work of Betty Lark-Horovitz in the early 1930s at the Cleveland Museum of Art. A *Seven Drawing Test* was used in the Museum's art classes as a screening and placement device. The test required subjects to complete seven specific drawing tasks, including drawing from memory, copying, and drawing from imagination. The results were graded with specific criteria and the grades were used to place participants in the Museum's advanced or average visual arts classes (Munro, Lark-Horovitz, and Barnhardt 1942).

A number of recently developed informal art instruments, based upon the work-sample technique, have been used as informal art tests in local visual arts programs or as related research instruments. Baker's *Visual Narrative Assessment* and *Visual Memory Assessment* instruments[1] were designed to identify visually gifted and talented students among applicants to The DeCordova Museum's Project Art Band in Lincoln, Massachusetts (Lazarus 1981). The *Visual Narrative Assessment* took the form of drawing done on a 12″ × 18″ sheet of paper with six rectangular preprinted frames. Subjects were asked, after preliminary warm-up, to follow the following instructions within forty minutes: "In the boxes on the large sheet of paper please draw some pictures that tell a story. Use as many boxes as you wish and if you need more sheets of paper you may have them." Upon completion, the visual narratives were assessed by a standardized scoring guide. The scoring guide (see Figure 23) was categorized into objects, composition, and story elements. Several trained judges scored the completed visual narratives to find students who acquire and utilize image-making abilities, have potential to be superior visual arts students, and to participate in a program for gifted and talented students. Figure 24 shows examples of drawings scored as below average, average, and above average responses from among the applicants who were administered Baker's *Visual Narrative Assessment*.

Baker's *Visual Memory Assessment* was administered by showing, and critically discussing for about ten minutes, a large reproduction of Vincent Van Gogh's *Bedroom at Arles*. The reproduction was removed from view and students then were asked to draw an accurate replication of the painting on a 12″ × 18″ sheet of drawing paper during a thirty minute period. The resulting drawings were rated by trained judges who scored the drawings on the basis of "quantitative and compositionally accurate recall" as indicators of giftedness as they reflected "accuracy of visual recall, retention of visual information, and ability to use such information in an altered manner." Scoring was quantified by specific recall and placement of objects shown in the original (see Figure 25). A scoring guide was used (see Figure 26) to quantify the results and subjects were assigned a single, numeric score. The results were considered, along with results obtained on a number of additional measures, as selection criteria for the DeCordova Museum's Project Art Band program. Figure 27 shows examples of drawings scored as below average, average, and above average from among the applicants who were administered Baker's *Visual Memory Assessment*.

Bellessis[2] has used the work-sample technique to assess the art abilities of students in her fifth-grade classes. She is a specialist art teacher who travels between three schools to teach art at upper elementary grades. Bellessis designed three drawing tasks for fifth-grade students that called for different complexes of art abilities including recall and originality, observation skills, and translation of an oral description into a drawing. These were a fantasy drawing, an observational drawing, and a dictated drawing. The fantasy drawing required students to: "Combine parts of three different animals into one, plausible new animal." The observational drawing, based upon a still life set up in the center of the classroom, required students to: "Draw what you see from where you are sitting, as realistically as possible." Dictated drawings were based upon hearing a teacher read a dictionary description of an aardvark, an animal most students would not have observed previously. The dictionary description was read, discussed, and read again and students were asked to: "Think about all of the characteristics I have just read and draw what you think this animal, an aardvark, looks like." Prior to each of these experiences, the teacher reviewed art elements and principles, size relationships, the depiction of values and textures, and other pertinent information students were expected to use in their drawings.

Each of four judges was trained individually to score the three types of drawings. Bellessis also discussed typical fifth grade drawing skills with the judges and used drawings obtained in a pilot study to establish categories of below average, average, and above average art students. Criteria used by the judges to score the fantasy, dictated, and still life drawings were degrees of success with balance in composition, line quality, texture, contrast, size and shape differences, pattern nuances, detail and elaboration, and suitableness of background.

In Figures 28, 29, and 30, three drawings representing below average, average, and above average responses to the fantasy, observational, and dictated drawing tasks are shown. These represent the range of abilities commonly found in heterogeneously grouped fifth-grade students. The disparity between the three levels of drawings are relatively typical and will be found in most classrooms.

The *Clark-Gareri Drawing Instrument*[3] has been used to assess drawing abilities of students who apply to the IU Summer Arts Institute. This instrument contains three drawing tasks, each on an $8\frac{1}{2}'' \times 11''$ page. Typed instructions, on the top of each page, direct applicants to draw in a prepared rectangle, make the best possible drawing, and:

1. draw a picture of an interesting house as if you were looking at it from across the street
2. draw a person running very fast
3. make a drawing of you and your friends playing in the school yard

Each page also included the sentence, "Use a #2 pencil and allow no more than 30 minutes for this drawing." There is a historical precedent for each of the three drawing tasks. Similar items have been used, though not in this particular grouping, in a number of studies from the past and discussions of their relevance and grading have appeared in the writing of researchers such as Thorndike (1913), Munro, Lark-Horovitz, and Barnhardt (1942), and Eisner (1967).

Before the items on the *Clark-Gareri Drawing Instrument* were administered to subjects, a Scoring Guide was developed (see Figure 31) and the instrument was administered to several groups of college and public school students. Results of the three drawing items were collected and scored, based on the Scoring Guide, to assess the effectiveness and accuracy of the Guide and to train judges. The Scoring Guide is detailed, but easy to use. Scores of one to five are assigned in relation to the use of sensory properties (line, shape, texture, value), formal properties (rhythm, balance, unity, composition), expressive properties (mood, originality), and technical properties (technique and craft and correctness of solution to the problem). The same Scoring Guide is used for each drawing and a total score is computed by adding scores received for each drawing. Because every subject is assigned the same tasks, in the same time frame, it is possible to compare results and rank order applicants on the basis of their total scores. This is the major advantage of the work-sample technique as compared to assessment of dissimilar art products created under uncontrolled conditions.

Examples of results with this instrument are shown in Figures 32, 33, and 34. In Figure 32, a below average, average, and above average drawing, all by eighth graders, are shown in response to Item 1 (draw a house as if you were looking at it from across the street). In Figure 33, a below average, average, and above average drawing, all by ninth graders, are shown in response to Item 2 (draw a person running very fast). In Figure 34, a below average, average, and above average drawing, all drawn by tenth graders, are shown in response to Item 3 (make a drawing of you and your friends playing in the school yard).

It should be noted that although all applicants to the IU Summer Arts Institute had been nominated as talented in the arts, their responses to the drawing tasks exhibit a wide range regarding drawing skills and abilities. This is not surprising; some applicants attend due to their interest in computer graphics, drama, dance, or music. An even greater range of abilities are found when these items are used with heterogeneously grouped students at various grades.

Informal art instruments generally are not trustworthy enough to be used as sole criteria for the selection of applicants into a visual arts program, because the criteria used for the scoring remain idiosyncratic. Informal art instruments will inevitably vary in quality and ability to predict success in a program, yet they can be valuable as part of a larger set of identification procedures.

Portfolio and performance review

The advantages of being able to view and critique each student's work and performance in person are obvious. Portfolio and performance review does have several drawbacks, however. Exclusive use of the procedure virtually eliminates identification of potential talent and, as practiced, such reviews are judged by local criteria that are often unknown to the applicants. Students who have taken prior arts classes obviously are advantaged in such review processes. Portfolio and performance reviews are costly to administer and time consuming. Candidates who have submitted portfolios or recorded performances also should be asked to create a related product under controlled conditions and while being observed by program judges. An advantage of portfolios is that they can display work in several media or related series of works; these are generally difficult to obtain in other ways. Having a student work with a variety of media, under controlled conditions, can give judges insight into a student's ability to use art skills and techniques and demonstrate expressive use of media.

Candidates to visual arts programs should be told, in advance, the specific portfolio requirements and criteria that will be used to judge the portfolios. It is unfair to ask for a portfolio and then reject a submission because it is atypical, too traditional, sparse, contains too many images, or for any other reason that is unknown to the candidates prior to their submissions.

Examples of criteria used for judging portfolios are shown in Figures 35 and 36. The sample Art Portfolio and Performance Review (Figure 35) outlines both required portfolio contents and the criteria that will be used to judge portfolios. It also includes information about additional performance requirements that will be requested from candidates who pass the portfolio review screening procedure. Figure 36 is an Art Product Evaluation Form that can be used to judge specific works in a portfolio, entire portfolio contents, or assess an art performance product. Both forms require training of judges to insure both similar interpretation of criteria and that all candidates are screened as equitably as possible.

Interviews

Interviews are conducted in a number of programs as an identification procedure following preliminary screening. Sometimes the interview is conducted at the same time portfolios or auditions are reviewed. Interviews give the applicant and interviewer chances to interact and share information in a non-structured, open-ended exchange. Interviews also should be used to give applicants information about the program as well as to collect information about the applicant that might not be available through other sources. Interviews are costly and time consuming, however, and should be used only as a *final* screening procedure.

Program designers should create interview protocols to assure that specific information derived from the interview will identify students that are best suited to the program offered. It is important that interviews be informal and relaxed, but that similar questions and topics are used with all candidates. A Self Evaluation Form (Figure 17) offers general questions of the kind that may be used in an interview. Interviews offer the opportunity for interviewers to get in-depth responses to questions that might not be included in written application materials.

Upon completion of an interview, a biographical inventory checklist (see Figure 37) can be used to summarize student responses in application packets and observations and interviews. Characteristics, similar to those found in Figure 37, have been shown to be highly correlated with other identification measures, accurately predict success in a program for artistically talented students, and do "not appear to be racially biased as opposed to the more traditional testing instruments" (Ellison, Fox, Coray, and Taylor 1981, p. 172). Interviewers should have opportunities to examine each candidate's application materials prior to each interview, in order to familiarize themselves with strengths, interests, goals, and other aspects expressed by the candidates in their application so that questions might be tailored to individual student interests.

Observations

Trained observers can be very accurate for identifying artistically talented students by observing students working in classrooms and other settings. It is important, sometimes, to observe students while they are creating art work or performing. Observing student behaviors, in general, yields a rich fund of information that would not be available from any other source. For example, the student who constantly draws and doodles on his or her notebook and school papers is indicating a burning desire to create images.

Observers should be persons who are objective and not regular participants in the classroom environment. Ideally, these observers should not come with any preconceived notions about the students or categories in which to classify the students' art talents. Information about students with talent and potential talent should emerge as the observer spends time in the classroom.

Many people have recommended observation as an important aspect of identification procedures. Observation, however, has two major limitations; it is costly and requires trained, perceptive observers who are not regular participants in the student's environment.

CONCLUSION

Most teachers who are interested in identifying talent in the visual arts want to be able, efficiently and effectively, to identify all possible talented students. Many students who are artistically talented, however, are not identified by procedures currently used in the schools. Most students do not take arts classes in later public school years and are not in school situations where they might be screened as talented.

There still are many limitations on objective identification of artistically talented students. There are no currently agreed-upon criteria based upon research findings that are reliable or valid for generalized use. This is why a diverse battery of procedures is highly recommended. Many questions remain to be answered about the important observable characteristics of art products and observable behaviors of students. Answers to these questions will guide future design of appropriate tests and procedures for the identification of artistically talented students. Procedures currently used, and others that are recommended for use, need to be critically examined and evaluated in light of research findings and successful implementation in the field.

NOTES

1. David W. Baker has given permission to publish his assessment instruments, examples of student responses, scoring sheets, and background information.

2. Martyna Bellessis has given permission to publish examples of student responses and background information about her study of children's art abilities.

3. Gilbert Clark and Charles Gareri have given permission to publish their drawing assessment instrument, its scoring guide, and examples of student responses. This instrument is still in a formative stage of development.

4

INSTRUCTIONAL MATERIALS

*O*NCE a group of artistically talented students has been identified for participation in a program, it is important to recognize that the degree and number of individual differences within this group will be equal to or greater than are found within
any other grouping of students. The common factors by which artistically talented students are identified for a program will not account for other factors that differentiate
them. Teachers of such groups, therefore, should be more sensitive to individual differences in terms of needs, abilities, and interests of students who are talented in the arts.
The wide variations that are found in groups of artistically talented students can be ac-
commodated best by individualizing all or part of their education through instructional
materials appropriate to their needs, abilities, and interests.

Many more instructional materials need to become available to art teachers
and talented art students, yet there *are* a number of diverse kinds of materials currently
available. Some were not designed specifically for artistically talented students but can
be used, or adapted for use, in school programs. The criteria used to assemble materials
for this chapter were that the materials generally were not used in schools, but were
commercially produced and thus readily available. As a result, locally produced, idiosyncratic resources, although they may be highly effective, are not reported. Another
selection criterion was *not* to include art media such as paper, paint, and clay because
these are commonly available and reported in catalogs from well known distributors.
Similarly, we avoided reference to films, filmstrips, textbooks, and classroom equipment because these materials are familiar to most art teachers. The only exceptions to
this selection criteria occurred when we felt an excellent source was not well known or
had been overlooked by most art teachers.

The categories listed for student-related and teacher-related instructional materials are not discrete; some materials listed fall into more than one category, although
they are only listed once. All instructional materials described and critiqued are representative *examples* of products to which we had access and do not include the entire
spectrum of available materials.

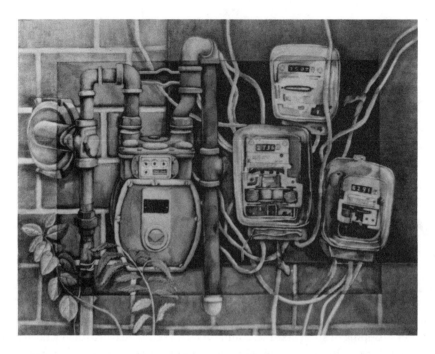

This watercolor painting was made by a tenth-grade boy in Plymouth High School in Plymouth, Indiana, who moved to the United States from China a year and a half before this picture was painted. His art education in China stressed developing technical skills and accurate observation. Photo by Joanna Ruhlman.

STUDENT-DIRECTED MATERIALS FOR INSTRUCTIONAL ENRICHMENT

Individualized instruction should derive and branch from an on-going curriculum that takes into account the abilities of talented students to learn a greater amount of material in a shorter period of time than other students in art classes. Such abilities make it possible to teach a greater breadth of content and approach some aspects of content in greater depth than is found in most art curricula. Because artistically talented students often want to learn many things, and many of them intensively, their teachers should have resources at hand and knowledge of access to resources in order to meet students' individual needs, abilities, and interests. In addition to greater numbers of general resources for learning, artistically talented students need materials that will challenge and expand their abilities. They should be directed to learning materials that go beyond typical curricula and encourage divergent thinking, problem solving, group decision making, and awareness and consideration of multiple alternatives. In addition, they need to learn higher level research skills involving problem analysis and criticism and development of advanced technical skills in relation to both studying and making art.

Khatena (1982) has pointed out that, "Sadly lacking in numbers are projects planned to provide for the nurture and development of talent in the many different areas of the visual and performing arts" (p. 420). In this chapter, we will present descriptions and critiques of instructional materials that can be used to supplement visual arts curricula at various grades and lead artistically talented students toward individualized development of their talents and abilities. Reviews of student-directed materials for instructional enrichment in this chapter have been grouped as workbooks and study guides, kits, games, and periodicals designed for students who are talented in the visual arts. Listings are organized in alphabetical order by author.

Workbooks and Study Guides

Animals: A Drawing Workbook, One of a Kind, P.O. Box 1393, Aspen, CO 81612

Many children who spend hours drawing outside their classrooms love to draw animals. One of a Kind has produced a drawing workbook that can be used as a sketchbook by groups of students or by individuals to record their animal drawings and research about animals.

Animals: A Drawing Workbook is a consumable product that introduces students to various methods and techniques of drawing, images by famous artists, and ideas about artists' drawings of animals. In a large format, with easy-to-read type and numerous illustrations, this workbook is divided into three parts. In part one, Animals Artists Know, students are directed to do observational drawings and research about animals. In part two, Animals Artists Imagine, users do research about style and composition and create a series of imaginary animals. In part three, More About Artists and Animals, students are directed to do research about animals and about art works that depict animals. They also learn related art vocabulary and drawing techniques. The workbook has a pocket on the inside back cover for the gathering of animal images. Four post-card-size reproductions, in color, are enclosed to begin the collection.

This drawing workbook is recommended for middle elementary through adult audiences. It is well-designed and suitable for enrichment activities for artistically talented students of all ages.

The illustrations are diverse, contemporary, and representative of many cultures from throughout the world. Although workbooks exist for many other subjects, this is one of the few that exist for the visual arts. The large text and reproductions make this workbook suitable for a younger audience.

Careers In Art: An Illustrated Guide, Brommer, Gerald, F. and Gatto, Joseph, A. (1984). Davis Publications, 50 Portland Street, Worcester, MA 01608

This book provides a great amount of useful information for anyone interested in visual arts careers. Art teachers, guidance counselors, parents, and administrators are often faced with questions from students such as, "How can I make a living as an artist?" *Careers in Art* provides an abundance of responses to this question. In our technological age, many artistically talented students are directed to study academic subjects or career-oriented subjects that do not include the visual arts. *Careers in Art* offers specific information to help guide students in their search for suitable career areas appropriate to their abilities in the visual arts.

The book is divided into seven sections that include information about a career area, descriptions of typical jobs, personal qualities needed for success in a visual arts career, alternative careers within an area, steps needed by high school students to prepare for an art career, and lists of college programs that provide pre-professional training. Each section features one or more Art Career Profiles, in which successful men and women are described in terms of typical tasks that they perform and specific aspects of their chosen careers. Fifteen major categories of careers are described and specific careers within each category are further discussed. The major categories are: architecture, interior and display design, graphic design, industrial design, fashion design, film and television, theater and stage design, editorial design and illustration, photography, fine art, crafts, art education, museums, art galleries, reporting and writing about art, and art services. The last section of the book is a compilation of resources including a bibliography, where to write for additional career information, and a complete listing of colleges and art schools by state that indicates which of eighteen career areas are offered.

Careers in Art contains valuable information that can be easily understood by high school students. The information covered is brief and generalized. Students interested in a specific career area can use the bibliography to find further information. We looked at the listing of major art career areas at Indiana University, where we teach, and found that our area, art education, was not checked. Neither were arts administration, fine arts, interior design, or theater arts design, though these career areas are all available on this campus. This raises some question about the accuracy of other information in the book.

Art/Design: Communicating Visually, Clark, Gilbert and Zimmerman, Enid. (1978). Art Education Incorporated, Blauvelt, NY 10913

Art/Design: Communicating Visually is an introductory, secondary level visual art textbook. The book's seven units are based upon study of the work of artists, art critics, art historians, and aestheticians. These units feature drawing, graphic design, printmaking, painting, sculpture, product design, and environmental design and are divided into four pairs of lessons in graded difficulty. A ninth lesson in each unit serves as a review and includes evaluation exercises. Because the lessons are graded, teachers can accommodate differing levels of ability within groups of art students. Students beginning the study of art and less advanced students might be expected only to complete the earlier lessons within each unit. More advanced art students might complete *all* lesson activities and evaluation exercises in the text. The teacher's manual that accompanies the text contains additional information about the lessons and additional evaluation exercises that can be used for students at all levels.

An unusual aspect of this text is that it contains lessons about art criticism, aesthetics, and art history that are equal in number to those about art-making. The content, therefore, helps develop student understanding about concepts related to art history, art criticism, aesthetics, and art making. The book is profusely illustrated and many learning activities are based directly upon analysis of the illustrations. Other illustrations exemplify artists' solutions to problems that are similiar to ones students are asked to solve. A number of repetitive African designs, for example, illustrate a lesson in which students are asked to create repeat-pattern designs.

Artistically talented students in earlier grades than high school could use this text as an independent, individualized workbook. The reading level is controlled and does not exceed middle-school level; upper elementary grade art students, with a good art vocabulary, would have no difficulty working independently with the book.

Portfolio Preparation Guide, Cote, Henry B. (1983). Visual/Technical Arts Department, Woonsocket Senior High School, 777 Cass Avenue, Woonsocket, RI 02895

Gifted and talented art students and their teacher from the Woonsocket, Rhode Island, Senior High School have prepared a booklet entitled *Portfolio Preparation Guide* to help themselves and other students prepare portfolios for critically evaluating their work, presenting their work to the public, and applying to many art-related jobs and art school and college art departments.

This thirty-eight-page booklet is one of more than a half dozen projects of the high school ASPIRE (Arts Shared by People Investing in Relevant Education) Program for visually gifted and talented students. *Portfolio Preparation Guide* was written by an ASPIRE art instructor, Henry Cote; four ASPIRE students created and edited the layout and calligraphy and arranged the booklet's numerous student and archival illustrations.

The booklet answers eight questions about portfolio preparation. Why should I prepare a portfolio? Where do I find ideas? What should I include? Which works should I choose? Who can help me? How shall I present my works? Where should I apply? When shall I submit my portfolio? Each of these questions is answered in a series of statements and illustrations designed to help students prepare portfolios for submission to Advanced Placement courses, college admissions, professional schools, or prospective employers.

There are several pages of student work from top-scoring portfolios. Specific directions for making a portfolio to hold artwork and mounting and labeling artwork and slides also are included. In a student-created publication such as this there is little money for high-quality printing, but the *Portfolio Preparation Guide* is of practical use to gifted and talented students who need guidance in the preparation and submission of a portfolio. The booklet is inexpensively duplicated and the quality of the illustrations suffers due to this factor. The hand-lettered pages are somewhat difficult to read, whereas the typed pages look more aesthetically pleasing and read more easily.

Dover Publications, Dover Publications, 180 Varick Street, New York, NY 10014

For many years Dover Publications has offered exceptional and unique educational resources for all teachers in the U.S. Teachers of artistically talented students should be aware of the numerous resources that Dover Publications offers for enrichment of learning about the arts. One of the most exciting is the many publications in the inexpensive "Pictorial Archives Series." These are copyright free images that can be reproduced or duplicated, in many ways, for educational purposes. Authentic Egyptian, Chinese, Aztec, American Indian, and other culturally derived images are available in the Pictorial Archive Series. Interested arts students who wish to use Pictorial Archive images in group or individual projects can choose from titles such as *Arabic Geometrical Pattern and Design; Art Nouveau: An Anthology of Design and Illustration from the Studio; African Designs from Traditional Sources; Costumes of the Greeks and Romans; Lettering and Layout; Symbols, Signs, and Signets; Allover Patterns for Designers and Craftsmen; Quaint Woodcuts in the Chapbook Style;* and *Women: A Pictorial Archive from Nineteenth Century Sources.* These varied themes and images can be used as sources of information, collage materials, intact resources, or teaching devices as visual references, and as blow-ups for various displays.

Coloring books, long neglected by teachers, are unique in the Dover catalog; their images are authentic. The images in such books as the *North American Indian Design Coloring Book, Visual Illusions Coloring Book,* or the *Mythical Beasts Coloring Book* can be used as classroom displays, posters, sources for fabric decoration, or as color theory lessons. Many Dover coloring books are also found in the Pictorial Archive Series.

In addition to these resources, Dover publishes inexpensive full color art books, architecture books, craft books, books about photography, and many titles that can help art students learn more about special areas of interest such as art history, commercial design, figure and animal drawings, architecture, costume, dolls and doll construction, graphic design, and natural subjects as sources for imagery.

A great number of titles apply to interests in lettering, layout, and advertising design. One of the resources for calligraphy students is examples of lettering from throughout history. The copying of letter designs from various periods of time is an exciting and demanding student task. So, too, is the copying of animals, figures, costumes, and implements from various periods of history. Dover offers innumerable visual resources for such exercises. If you are interested in any of the Dover titles, be sure to state that you want a full catalog and that you want to be placed on the Dover Publications Inc. mailing list.

Wassily Kandinsky, Grassinger, Stephany (1982). Zephyr Press, 430 South Essex Lane, Tucson, AZ 85711

Wassily Kandinsky is one of Zephyr Press' Self-Directed Study units that were developed for gifted and talented students in elementary and middle schools. The book's pages are designed to be reproduced for classroom use and offer choices among various learning activities. There are two sets of pages, one for students in grades K through three and another for students in grades four through eight.

A brief, one-page introduction to the life and work of Kandinsky is offered as A Word To The Teacher and a list of materials needed to complete the activities in this unit are all the teacher resources offered. Students are led, with one-page activity sheets, to self-directed activities that are meant to develop inquiry skills, knowledge, and understanding of the life and work of Wassily Kandinsky.

Eight high-quality slides of non-objective art works by Kandinsky are bound into the study guide. No mention, however, is made about how to use them or where they should be studied in the unit. The book's pages are hand lettered and illustrated, but no images by Kandinsky are offered in the text. Some of the inquiry activities, such as "Choose at least two paintings by Wassily Kandinsky and DISCUSS them with a group of students and a teacher" are good starting points for learning activities but lack the criteria needed for successful completion. Unless a teacher has adequate knowledge about Kandinsky and is willing to guide the student activities suggested in the unit, students may have fun but will not learn about Kandinsky and the art works he created.

Drawing and Storytelling: A Study Guide for Art 23A, Hoff, Gary. (1984). Independent Study Program, Indiana University, Bloomington, IN 47405

Offering independent learning activities is a common recommendation for the education of artistically talented students. *Drawing and Storytelling* is specifically an independent study guide currently being used as a high school art text. The emphasis is upon narrative drawing, often described as visual storytelling. The study guide's contents and lessons were developed while the author was teaching a visual narrative class for a number of years as part of the Indiana University Summer Arts Institute.

Drawing and Storytelling can be used for group and independent activities in the classroom. Narrative drawing is commonly recognized as a popular form of spontaneous art expression by artistically talented young people. This study guide is one of a few efforts to specifically address the teaching of skills related to creating visual narratives.

Drawing and Storytelling is copiously illustrated by the author, other artists, and former students of the author. There are nine lessons, a sketchbook, and a final project required when the study guide is used in conjunction with the independent study program. In lesson one, a brief history of narrative art is presented and the work of artists from the past are introduced. A variety of drawing materials and how they are used is discussed in lesson two. The cornerstone of narrative art, how to draw the human figure including foreshortening and perspective, form the content of lesson three. In lesson four, similarities and differences between portraits and caricatures are explored. The first lessons in storytelling begin in lesson six and continue through lesson nine. Topics such as cartooning, embellishment, lettering, and layout are presented as means of creating powerful, visually unified narratives.

This award-winning study guide is written for high school level students and easily can be used independently. The study guide has a great appeal for artistically talented students who often spend a great deal of their own time creating visual narratives. The layout is handsome and the numerous high quality illustrations compliment the text. The visual narratives included in this study guide will appeal to junior high and high school age students because so many of them were created by students their own age.

Art Synectics, Roukes, Nicholas. (1982). Davis Publications, Inc., Printer's Building, Worcester, MA 01608

Often talented art students need ideas and inspiration to bring forth new forms of expression that are neither trite or stereotyped. *Art Synectics,* by Nicholas Roukes, provides simulating and contemporary projects based upon bringing diverse unrelated objects, ideas, and images into unified connections.

Students using this book are encouraged to transform common elements, through mixing and matching, to create visual metaphors and analogues. The author claims that the student must use "intuitive intelligence" that is based upon emotional, psychological, and rational factors that allow feelings and perceptions to be expressed visually.

This book contains 126 project activities and is divided into six chapters: Analogy; Imaging and Transforming; Signals, Signs, and Symbols; Myth and Myth Making; Ritual, Game, and Performance; and Paradox. Each chapter contains a brief discussion related to major concepts and a series of exercises, games, and activities that emphasize studio experiences related to the chapter's title. The chapters are copiously illustrated; there are 215 black and white images that emphasize such themes as symbolism, psychological drama, fantasy, and dream-like contexts.

The book concludes with a section titled Art Synector: The Artists Think Tank, designed to prod the student's imagination by bringing together highly disparate elements. Students select, by chance, three diverse terms from a list of one hundred and are required to reconcile them by using these terms and creating an image in any appropriate media.

Art Synectics is intended for junior and senior high school students and is being used in a number of gifted and talented visual art programs around the country. This book would be especially useful as a resource to stimulate creative thinking in the visual arts but not as a complete curriculum due to its limited emphasis on art-making activities related to synectics.

Kits

Ancient Egyptian Art and Architecture (EE103), Alarion Press, P.O. Box 1882, Boulder, CO 80306

Alarion Press offers a series of sound filmstrip kits in its history through art and architecture series. These kits explain and analyze art and architecture of the past and draw comparisons with the present. Different kinds of kits are designed for students in grades four to nine, high school, and adult audiences. Alarion Press stresses the use of these kits with gifted and talented students due to their subject matter, in-depth content, and emphasis on individualized learning. These kits are intended for interdisciplinary learning and can be used for social studies, language arts, or art classes as well as for gifted and talented education.

Each kit contains filmstrips and cassettes, a wall poster, an illustrated teacher's manual with a script of the narration and identification of filmstrip frames, a timeline, projects and activities related to the content, and quizzes that may be reproduced for students to use. At present, kits are available about Egyptian, Greek, Roman, Byzantine, Medieval, and Renaissance art and architecture.

An example of these kits, Ancient Egyptian Art and Architecture for Middle School grades, features two filmstrips and two cassettes. The first cassette and filmstrip explain why and how the Egyptians built tombs, pyramids, and temples. The other cassette and filmstrip discuss wall paintings and portraiture in ancient Egypt.

The teacher's manual is very well illustrated, contains the full text of the cassettes, and identifies all the images shown on the filmstrips. In addition, it contains seven reproducable pages of drawings and text that elaborate upon concepts previously presented in the filmstrip. These pages also suggest learning activities and extension activities for interested students. An excellent glossary of terms and a bibliography of additional sources that students can use to help guide inquiry also are included. A final feature, important for resource libraries and school resource centers, is a full set of file cards for cataloguing the kit.

The Alarion Press kits are designed to appeal to their audiences and are well packaged. These resources can be used to bring historical understanding to students, but would need greater amplification than is offered in art making, art criticism, and aesthetics, three areas of study important for a well-rounded art education. Some full color study prints should be used to supplement the black and white drawings offered in the kit.

Art Institute of Chicago Junior Museum, Museum Store, Art Institute of Chicago, Michigan at Adams, Chicago, IL 60603

Not every artistically talented student is fortunate enough to live near a great art museum and have opportunities to view its collection. Some museums, however, are attempting to make their collection more accessible by creating educational materials and publications. An excellent example of such efforts is a series of packets available from the Junior Museum of the Art Institute of Chicago.

Scrutinizing Art, This Colorful World, What is American About American Art?, Native Arts, and *Art That Works* are examples of recently developed packets of study materials. *Scrutinizing Art* is a general introduction to the Art Institute of Chicago. It consists of an illustrated booklet, fifteen color postcards of art reproductions, and numerous study questions and activities that introduce major art objects from the museum's collection. In *This Colorful World,* Impressionist artists and their ideas are discussed in an illustrated activity folder and sixteen color postcards illustrate major Impressionist paintings and drawings from the museum's collection. *What Is American About American Art?* is a packet that illustrates the wide range of American art by emphasizing the work of nineteen famous American artists. Color reproductions and black and white illustrations guide the student through an examination of American art themes and figures. *The Native Arts* packet presents art from Peru, West Africa, the American Southwest, and the South Pacific. Observation, discussion, and activity suggestions are offered for each of the native cultures. *Art That Works* includes an illustrated booklet, filmstrip, and poster that introduce crafts and decorative arts that are functionally useful. Historical and contemporary craft objects and period rooms are illustrated with provocative study questions and suggested activities. Each Junior Museum packet includes a useful bibliography for further inquiry by students.

Teachers who visit the Art Institute of Chicago can receive these well-illustrated packets, without charge, if they arrange guided tours for students. Teachers in other parts of the country can order the packets and use them for group lessons or for individualized study materials for gifted and talented students. Some of the packets, open on three sides, may need to be repackaged to prevent loss and misplacement of materials.

Cu ra'tor Express, Zephyr Press, 430 South Essex Lane, Tucson, AZ 85711

Cu ra'tor Express is an art appreciation program, in the form of a kit, that can be used to involve students in a research project with famous works of art. It can be used with small groups or an entire class and is appropriate for elementary and junior high students. Teams of students, using the kit, compete to create the most interesting and informative art exhibit. In the process of producing an art exhibit, students learn to classify art works by subject matter, style, chronological order, or media. They also do library research about artists, art styles, and art in historical contexts. The program requires that students prepare a lecture about their team's exhibition in progress and enhance their exhibits with extra materials such as slides, lighting, and background music. Posters designed to advertise each team's exhibition must be based on the style of one or more of the paintings in the exhibit. For each of these activities, points are awarded by the teacher, and outside judges if possible, and the winning team is announced. There are nine optional activities that extend and enrich the *Cu ra'tor Express* program. These activities can be done individually as well as in groups. Teachers of artistically talented students could add additional optional activities and resources to the kit.

Included in the kit are a teacher's guide, twenty post-card size art reproductions, student and team logs, posters directing the activities and optional activities, a student classification form, and a guide for judging the team's exhibitions. The twenty art reproductions are selected to represent major periods, styles, and subject matters. By participating in this program, students are introduced to twenty important artists, visual arts vocabulary, library resources, and skills of team work using art categories and organizers.

This is one of the few resources for introducing art history, art criticism, and aesthetics at an experiential level appropriate for elementary school students. *Cu ra'tor Express* was created by Charlotte Jaffe, a teacher-coordinator of gifted education programs in New Jersey. In her words, "cu ra'tor is an outgrowth of my experience in devising art history programs for hundreds of students in both gifted and regular classrooms." Activities are designed to involve students in interaction in terms of decision making about aesthetic attributes, critical qualities, and historical aspects of works of art. The materials are designed to appeal to students and directions are easy to follow.

The twenty reproductions are not of a high quality and the color of the borders, upon which they are printed, distracts from the colors found in the reproductions. Teachers with access to museum-quality post cards can replace the reproductions with other sets that could be grouped to teach similar or different concepts than those suggested in *Cu ra'tor Express*.

Jackdaw Learning Packages, Longman Incorporated, Schools Division, 19 West 44th Street, New York, NY 10036

A jackdaw is a glossy, black crow. Jackdaw is also the trade name of an extensive series of social studies learning packages published in England, Canada, and the United States. Each Jackdaw is a compilation of about eleven color and black-and-white reproductions of original historical documents related to a specific theme, with illustrated broadsheets that extend the documents, offer translations, and suggest related learning activities. There are over 150 different topics, ranging from historical events, famous people and places, social movements, games and holidays, to natural phenomena. Many Jackdaws provide excellent opportunities for individualized art projects using inexpensive learning materials. Artistically talented students might use such Jackdaws as Tutankhamun; China: A Cultural Heritage; Hadrian's Wall; Caxton and the Early Printers; and The Mayflower and the Pilgrim Fathers to learn about sculpture, architecture, printmaking, calligraphy, product design, and graphic design.

Many Jackdaws contain heavy paper sheets that can be cut and constructed to form models of such things as buildings, three-dimensional scenes, objects, and experimental devices or to be used as dramatic posters. Other objects unique to each topic, such as vinyl phonograph records, are occasionally included.

Every Jackdaw package is 9″ × 13½″ × ¼″ and printed on washable plastic fabric. This size and durability make for easy storage, accessibility, and classroom performance. Jackdaw titles offered in the United States are listed in a catalogue printed by Longmans. A general guide for using Jackdaws in the classroom and a durable storage box also can be obtained from the same company.

Jackdaw packages contain many interesting and varied materials that may require additional information for students not accustomed to individualized instruction. The packages can be supplemented with materials such as teacher-prepared questions and problems, student worksheets, and past student work. Since Jackdaws are designed for use in social studies classes, additional art visuals and sheets directed toward art learnings would be appropriate.

Games

ART DECK: The Game Of Modern Masters, Impressionism To Surrealism, Aristoplay, Ltd., 931 Oakdale Road, P.O. Box 7645, Ann Arbor, MI 48107

ART DECK is a game based upon a typical, fifty-two playing-card deck; there are four suits and the standard sequence of Ace to King cards in each suit. Each card is also printed with a small art reproduction; thirteen artists and four images by each artist are used to represent changes in style from Impressionism to Surrealism. There are, in addition, thirteen "artist" cards that provide an artist's name, date and place of birth and death, a style name, a very brief description of the artist's career, and a listing of four titles of art works used in the set. There is a die, used in the play, a set of rules, and an index booklet indicating image titles and their sources. There are also four card holders to be used by players.

Play consists of creating sets of related cards as in rummy or canasta; three to four cards of paintings by the same artist are also matching number cards (four aces are four Miro cards, etc.). Playing series in the same suit (three, four, five of spades, etc.) creates a set in which the artist or images are scrambled without consistency to any visual commonality. "Artist" cards are used to match sets of images for play and are also used for bonus points.

The quality of reproduction on the cards is excellent, although all the images are placed to be seen correctly while holding a card hand. As a result, large rectangular, horizontal paintings are shown as smaller images than rectangular, vertical paintings.

A major criticism of *ART DECK* is its lack of clarity about purpose. It is a hybrid mix of art content and traditional playing cards. As an art-content, educational game it has great potential. As it replicates more typical rummy rules, it loses track of its purpose as an art-related learning device. All of the sets (four images by one artist) are, in fact, matching numerals across suits. As a result, players can match numerals and therefore play a set of four Queens and not be aware that it is also a set of four images by Kandinsky. The artists used in the game are Miro, Monet, Degas, Renoir, Seurat, Gauguin, Van Gogh, Cézanne, Braque, Picasso, Kirshner, Kandinsky, and Klee. These are all well-known, Western Eruopean, male artists. Addition of American and women artists would make the images more global and communicate to students that American and women artists also contributed to art history from Impressionism and Surrealism.

The *ART DECK* cards can be used to create new games and tasks not included in the directions. It would be challenging to ask gifted and taiented students to create new games and new sets of rules using the cards in this set. *ART DECK* is a well packaged game and would be easy to store and use in a classroom. Like all kits, games, and packaged resourced in general, it would be important that players repackage the box after use to replace all the component parts.

Design Game, The Krannert Art Museum, University of Illinois at Champaign-Urbana, Urbana, IL 61801

Since 1971, the Krannert Art Museum, on the University of Illinois campus, has been distributing the *Design Game*. This game is an effective package of simple, manipulative materials that can be used to teach basic design elements to young students. As designed, the *Design Game* is used to acquaint pre-kindergarten, kindergarten, and primary grade museum visitors with basic color, shape, line, and texture concepts and vocabulary. The game may be played with any type of art object found in the usual art museum or art exhibition.

This package is a simple four-part fold-out with four sleeves that hold color, shape, line, and texture cards. Color cards are 5″ square and are red, yellow, blue, green, orange, and purple. Shape cards are about the same size and are a triangle, oval, rectangle, circle, and square. The line cards are white, 5″ squares with press-type lines that are straight, diagonal, zigzag, scalloped, undulating, and curved. Texture cards, also 5″ square, are covered with gold or silver metallic, velveteen, satin, lace, simulated wood, or coarse sandpaper textures.

Instructions call for students to examine each card, name it, and relate its concept to everyday objects such as matching the cards to objects in the immediate environment. In this way, the vocabulary of basic design elements is learned and experienced in the everyday environment. Museum visitors are asked to match the cards to art objects on exhibition. For example, students with a red color card or zigzag line card are asked to find a museum art object with red color or zigzag lines. In the classroom, this activity could be used with art reproductions or other stimulus objects.

Although this game was designed for young children, students of various ages who are gifted in art would enjoy using the cards in a variety of ways. The package can be used for individual study to trigger the identification of art elements. Questions such as, you have the blue card, how many shades of blue can you identify in this painting? Or you have a curved line card, how many different curved lines can you identify in this sculpture? An interesting studio experience would be to give one color, shape, line, and texture card and direct the student to create a design based upon variations of only these four elements. Gifted students could be asked to create game tasks for other students. Teachers can use this game as a model for creating other art games to be used by their students in both individual and group situations.

The materials are very sturdy, large and simple, and easy to manipulate. They are coded for easy repackaging. The box that contains the fold-out holder makes it easy to store and retrieve the game. A drawback is that the game pieces will fall out of the holder if it is not held correctly.

Collector's Choice: The Impressionists, One of a Kind, P.O. Box 1393, Aspen, CO 81612

One of a Kind offers interesting card games, drawing workbooks, posters, and kits about art that can be used in classrooms. Each product combines introductory concepts, information about famous artists and art movements, and challenging learning activities. They are appropriate independent activities as well as group activities.

Of special interest for talented students studying the visual arts is a card game, *Collector's Choice: The Impressionists.* This game introduces young players to the works of Renoir, Cassett, Degas, and Monet. It also presents information about these artists and asks Collector's Questions that help young people acquire knowledge about the Impressionist Movement and about styles, compositions, and subject matters used by these artists. The game is easy to play; it requires not much more skill than Old Maid and can be played many times without loss of interest. There are eight blank cards that can be filled in by teachers or other users to extend the game's content or appropriateness to specific groups or users, such as artistically talented students.

The deck has sixty-four cards: sixteen signature cards that present information about each artist; thirty-two art reproduction cards of works by Renoir, Cassatt, Degas, and Monet; and eight Collector's Question Cards with questions and eight blank question cards. The game is played by two to six players who must trade and collect four sets of cards about each artist.

In this game the art reproductions are of high quality and durability. A small cardboard box would make a more suitable package for shelf storage than the plastic packaging in which it is now offered.

MELD games: Artifacts, Visual Dominoes, Artery, Articulation, M.E.L.D., ℅ Eldon Katter, 464 East Walnut Street, Kutztown, Pa 19530

Like most children, gifted and talented students enjoy playing games. In fact, many gifted and talented children collect and play games more actively and seriously than other children. *Artifacts, Visual Dominoes, Artery,* and *Articulation* are four games for students designed to increase visual perception skills, teach sensitivity to basic art history concepts, and awareness of visual similarities among art images.

Artifacts is a boxed set of fifty-four black-and-white illustrations of cars, telephones, chairs, women's hats, architectural details, and pocket watches produced from 1890 to 1970; fifty-four descriptive cards, fifty-four time factor cards, and a set of rules and playing pieces. The game can be played on several levels for different age groups, from simple grouping tasks to complex historical categorizations based upon stylistic attributes. Time factor cards, for instance, describe economic, social, political, popular arts, and technological aspects of six major time periods from 1890 to 1970. These are used, in the advanced games, to simulate an art historian's study of events of the past to date, interpret, and explain the visual characteristics of historical objects.

Advanced play includes ordering the six types of images in chronological sequences and matching object, descriptive, and time factor cards in ways that require group discussions and resolution of errors. This activity is fun; it also teaches players to interpret the significance of observable characteristics of objects as evidence of historical contexts.

Visual Dominoes is a simple game that is infinitely variable. The designers, in fact, encourage teachers, students, parents, or whoever plays the game to add new dominoes by cutting images from magazines and mounting these on index cards to extend the visual features used in play. Matching visual characteristics, end-to-end, develops a visual matrix that each player must justify as the play progresses. In other words, if a player is matching by texture, color, shape, or any other visual similarity, this must be announced and accepted by other players as the game goes on. The designers provide two 8½" × 11" printed sheets, that can be cut into twelve playing pieces, to begin the domino set. The object of the game is to build a visually interesting matrix based upon recognizing basic visual similarities between dissimilar images. The play, obviously, can be at relatively simple to relatively sophisticated levels.

Artery is a board game that requires identification of design elements, style, composition, and subject matter as found in twenty-five post card reproductions. There are forty-four descriptive word cards that teach art vocabulary and art concepts and six sets of colored chips that are used to tally each player's score.

Players must match descriptive word cards to visual characteristics of art reproductions. Matched descriptive word cards and reproductions must be agreed upon
by all players before play proceeds. As a result, discussion reinforces the concepts
taught on the descriptive word cards. Game strategy requires thought and planning by
each player.

A variation of the *Artery* game is *Auction Gallery* where the same cards are
used to "bid" on works of art. All picture cards are shown face up and players must
match three different description cards to bid on a work of art which he or she may
collect. Bids may be challenged by other players leading again to discussion about the
attributes of works of art.

Articulation is a gallery game in instructional kit form that includes three
games that can be played with the same equipment. It is a board game for three to five
players that uses post-card reproductions of art works as a major component. *Articulation* requires debate that allows students to analyze art works from varying points of
view, verbalize their conclusions about art works, and support their conclusions with
argument and evidence about design elements, the humanities, and aesthetic responses.
This game requires players to present and weigh competing evidence and arguments
about works of art for an extended time and as a sequential activity. Tasks are simple at
first and become more complex as the play progresses.

Socially, the activities range from individually-oriented to group-oriented activities. At the outset of the game, individual players make independent decisions. As
the game progresses, individuals begin to compete against other individuals. Eventually, all players must reach a consensus, and together form a collective opinion.

All MELD games are well packaged, inexpensive, and attractive. They represent an attempt to improve instruction about responses to art in direct, useable, practical forms. Students learn to make group decisions about complex issues without ap-
pealing to the authority of the teacher. Directions for the games are sometimes difficult
to understand due to complex explanations and poor reproduction quality.

Periodicals For Students

Art to Zoo, Smithsonian Institution, Office of Elementary and Secondary Education,
Washington, DC 20560

The Smithsonian Institution offers a school newsletter published four times a
year entitled *Art to Zoo*. This handsome publication contains articles about a variety
of topics (with a major theme each issue) that are related to the art and artifact collections in a dozen national museums. Articles about topics as diverse as Victorian architecture, zoo design, and Eskimo masks appear each year. Suggested activities, information about related educational materials, and bibliographies related to the theme
accompany the illustrated articles. Each issue contains a pull-out page that can be used
to direct individual inquiry into each issue's theme. Art content and many illustrations
suitable for display are integral parts of each issue.

Art to Zoo is of invaluable assistance for art teachers who want to use mu-

This linoleum block print was made by an eighth-grade student in the IU Summer Arts Institute, after studying numerous reproductions of wood cuts and linoleum block prints by well-known artists. This image is based on observations of tropical plants in the Indiana University greenhouse. Photo by Indiana University AV Services.

seums, parks, zoos, and other atypical resources in their communities to challenge their gifted and talented students. Students who do not have immediate access to these atypical resources will benefit from reading and using activities in *Art to Zoo*. With access to the collections of over ten national museums, the resulting illustrations are of high quality and good examples for students to study.

Challenge: Reaching and Teaching the Gifted Child, Good Apple, Inc., Box 299, Carthage, IL 62321

    Challenge is a bi-monthly magazine, published five times per year, that is directed to parents, teachers, and gifted children from kindergarten to eighth grade. The contents are varied in each issue although topics of identification, evaluation, methods of instruction, learning materials, model programs, and mind teasers are featured.

    Challenge is addressed to gifted education in general and includes articles about science, literature, social science, etc. The arts are included, although not featured. Recent issues have had articles about the aesthetics of architecture, advertising, and similar topics. Most of the articles in the magazine offer teaching suggestions including specific activities to use with students.

    Each issue contains a two-month calendar with activity suggestions on each day's entry. This feature is entitled Just Think ... and the activities listed are thought provoking and interesting. Many of the articles are units about particular topics and activities, some are general information, and some are games or puzzlers.

The magazine illustrations often are free, public-access images from sources such as Dover Publications and often do not illustrate, as much as decorate, the articles. The graphic design of the magazine is not consistent with the quality of the articles presented in *Challenge.*

Chart Your Course! By and For Creative Students, Chart Your Course. G/T/C Publishing Company, P.O. Box 6448, Mobile, AL 36660

Chart Your Course is a magazine, published eight times a year, containing materials created by gifted and talented students for all children to read and enjoy. Cartoons, reviews, songs, articles, puzzles, photographs, comic strips, interviews, stories, art work, poems, activities, editorials, plays, and other original work by students from primary through high school grades are included in this magazine. Some regular features include art work, plays, just for fun, poetry, prose, pen pals, music, cartoons, and photography.

Chart Your Course presents a rare opportunity for young people who are talented in the visual arts to publish their art work for a nationwide audience. All work must be original and labeled with the student's name, birth-date, school, and home address. Illustrations, cartoons, comics, and other forms of drawing must be clear and drawn in black ink. Glossy clear photographs and 35mm transparancies are acceptable if original work cannot be mailed easily.

Chart Your Course has a familiar children's magazine layout with many adult-drawn cartoon-like characters scattered throughout the written materials. The student drawings in the magazine are a refreshing addition and enhance the stories, poems, and activities written by other students. A student color photograph is used on the cover of each issue of the magazine and sometimes a few color photographs are found within its pages. More visuals by students should be used to accompany the written materials and they should replace many of the cartoon drawings that look as if they could be found in any children's magazine.

This magazine should definitely appeal to all young people, especially those who like to see the work of their peers in print. The activities are challenging, especially for intermediate and junior high school students. One student wrote to the editor: " 'Chart Your Course!' is really great for all ages, 3 to 88! Plenty of things for you to do, puzzles, games and stories too! Just read this magazine and you'll have fun. Read "Chart Your Course." It's number one!" (October, 1985 issue.)

PRISM: A Magazine for the Gifted, Prism Publishing, 900 East Broward Boulevard, Fort Lauderdale, FL 33301

PRISM is a new magazine that explores the work, thoughts, and aspirations of gifted and talented students. This magazine is directed toward an intermediate, junior and senior high school audience although parents, teachers, and administrators will find it informative and interesting. There has been little opportunity for gifted students to see their creations published or to create a network with other gifted young people. The editors of *PRISM* see this magazine as a vehicle not only for publication of work by gifted students, but also as the beginning of a communication network among gifted and talented students. Experts in the field of gifted and talented education and adults also contribute to *PRISM*.

In *PRISM*'s first issue, autobiographical articles about growing up gifted, poetry and brief essays by gifted and talented students, reports about gifted and talented programs and achievements of students in special programs, photographs, drawings, and illustrations by artistically talented students, book reviews, and several pages of "Pen Pals" noting names, addresses, and special interests are presented. Math, science, philosophy, history, literature, the future, personal experiences, humor, and current events are all topics about which the editors encourage young gifted and talented people to write. In addition, photographs and art work are invited as illustrations for the magazine. Teachers of artistically talented students may want to encourage their students to submit art work to this magazine.

The *PRISM* editorial team encourages comments and contributions from gifted and talented students, teachers of gifted and talented students, and parents with gifted and talented children. Submissions are directed toward an announced theme and may include ideas, letters to the editor, fiction or non-fiction articles, poems, illustrations, and photography. As the magazine continues to publish, the quality of student contributions should become more consistently represented at a high level that demonstrates contributions of gifted and talented students in our country's schools.

TEACHER-DIRECTED MATERIALS FOR INSTRUCTIONAL ENRICHMENT

Teachers of artistically talented students need instructional materials that differ from those commonly used for general instructional purposes. One crucial factor in effective educational programs is knowledgeable and sympathetic teachers who can guide the many forms of talent that will appear in any grouping of artistically talented students. A generalized understanding of gifted and talented educational programs and students and a specialized understanding of artistically talented students are both required. Another required skill is ability to guide students' independent or individualized instruction; this requires knowledge of and access to instructional materials that can be used by groups and individual students appropriate to their needs for instruction and inquiry. Reviews of teacher-directed materials for instructional enrichment, presented in this chapter, are organized into books about teaching gifted and talented students, books and periodicals about teaching artistically talented students, books with background information, and catalogs and media services. Also included are a generalized resource-source list that can be used to obtain a myriad of additional materials and a section about creating teacher-made instructional materials.

Books and Periodicals
About Teaching Gifted and Talented Students

Developing Talent In Young People, Bloom, Benjamin S. (Ed.). (1985). Ballantine Books, 201 E. 50th Street, New York, NY 16022

With so many pressing questions about the development of talent in young people unanswered, this book is of major importance. The content is based upon intensive study of 120 young people who had reached world-class levels of attainment in particular areas of the arts, sports, science, or mathematics and who were willing to share their life stories with the researchers. Some selection criteria were particularized within each specialization; the sculptors, for instance had to have been awarded a Guggenheim Fellowship or the Rome Prize for their work. Another criterion included being born and reared in the United States in order for the researchers to study teaching and learning processes within one country. Youth also was required; nearly all subjects were below the age of thirty-five when they were interviewed in order to insure clear recollection of earlier experiences and increase the possibility of access to parents and past teachers who also would be interviewed.

Members of the research project identified individuals who met their criteria as top-level pianists, sculptors, Olympic swimmers, tennis players, research mathematicians, or research neurologists. Of these, eighteen to twenty-one individuals within each category were available and agreed to participate. Thus 120 individuals, their parents, and selected teachers were interviewed to gain a picture of how talent, in each of these diverse fields, emerges and is developed. In various chapters of this book, each category of individuals is described as a distinct group and one pianist, swimmer, and mathematician are described as particular case studies. Other chapters integrate the findings of the project across categories and describe phases of learning, home influences, the effect of commitment to learning, and other generalizations about the development of talent.

Bloom, the editor, points out that neither potential nor precociousness are sufficient to insure talent development. "No matter what the initial characteristics (or gifts) of the individuals, unless there is a long and intensive process of encouragement, nurturance, education, and training, the individuals will not attain extreme levels of capability" (p. 3). The editor also notes that rarely have these individuals "progressed far enough by age eleven or twelve for anyone to make confident predictions that they would be among the top twenty-five in (their) talent field by the ages of twenty or thirty" (p. 533). The book describes talent development as a complex, multi-faceted, and laborious process that demands a long-term committment and dedication.

The book's description of three phases of development, the early, middle, and later years, common to all the individuals studied, is a major contribution. These phases are not age specific and vary greatly for pianists or sculptors, for instance, but characterize an essential pattern for talent development and its nurturance.

All teachers and parents of gifted and talented students should read *Developing Talent In Young People*. It will surprise, shock, and disturb readers who believe gifted and talented students can make it on their own. That the opposite is true, they cannot, is amply documented in this book; the critical, crucial roles parents, teachers, coaches, and other mentors must play are made apparent.

Unfortunately, the development of talent of young sculptors is analyzed less thoroughly than other categories of achievement. They are less likely to show early promise, make their commitment at a later age, and come into contact with the kinds of teachers and student-peers needed for their development only as young adults. Their development is recognized as atypical from the other categories of talent described, but it also is noted that their development pattern and the support systems needed in their development are essentially the same as in the other fields. Obviously, more needs to be done, specifically in relationship to studying painters, jewelers, ceramicists, print-makers, and other visual arts specializations. A model has been created and reported in this very important book; there is more, however, to be learned about the development of talent in the visual arts.

Developing Talent In Young People should be read by every educator and parent concerned with the education of gifted and talented students. The clarity of the writing and copious quotations from the remarkable young people and their parents who contributed to this study are delightful to read. They provide insights about talent development that simply have not been available until now.

G/C/T, G/C/T Publishing Company, P.O. Box 6448, Mobile, AL 36660

G/C/T is advertised as the "world's most popular magazine for parents and teachers of gifted, creative, and talented children." This magazine contains groups of articles related to specific topics, feature articles, and departmental colums. It is directed more toward parents of academically gifted students than those talented in the arts. Topics are varied and designed to be helpful for parents and teachers who work with gifted and talented students. Identification, motivation, curriculum, program descriptions, sibling rivalry, inter-family relationships, recollections of adults who were gifted and talented children, rural gifted, and guiding the gifted female are among the many topics that have appeared in the magazine since 1978.

Conference announcements, reviews of books, and advertisements for educational products including games and kits are also found in this magazine. The articles are timely and written in a popular form for parents and teachers. Many contain suggestions that can be used in homes and schools to help guide gifted and talented students. *G/C/T* has high quality illustrations and an interesting format.

Of special interest are articles about adults as models for achievement and success in a variety of careers. For instance, a recent issue featured McArthur Fellows, a group of people with an enormous range of abilities who were selected to receive financial awards to support their research and activities. These Fellows responded to a questionnaire that asked them to recall several aspects of their academic and extra-curricula school activities. Their responses can help students, teachers, and parents understand the motivation and characteristics of students who may some day become leaders as independent thinkers, researchers, and artists.

From examination of a six year index (1978 to 1984), it is apparent that few articles have appeared about the visual and performing arts or that address the needs of students who are talented in the arts. It also appears that the editors are willing to publish such material were it to be submitted.

Providing Programs for the Gifted and Talented: A Handbook, Kaplan, Sandra N. (1974). The National/State Leadership Training Institute in Gifted and Talented, Civic Center Tower Building, Suite PH-C, 316 West Second Street, Los Angles, CA 90012

Have you been thinking of a gifted and talented program for your school, but just can't seem to get started? Now there's help. *Providing Programs for the Gifted and Talented: A Handbook,* by Sandra Kaplan, discusses issues and provides worksheets and models that can be duplicated and used in group planning sessions. Although there are no suggestions that are specific to programs for artistically talented students, the discussions and models are appropriate for general G/T program planning. You need only to adapt the suggestions and models to the special needs of artistically talented students.

Topics and decisions basic to G/T program planning, such as philosophy, identification, school services, and program goals are discussed. The handbook presents various program prototypes, then it gives guidelines for curriculum development and instructional services. The last part of the book deals with developing written plans and implementing your own program.

This handbook is relevant for people who are initiating or expanding a program for gifted and talented students. It is a practical guide that provides alternative solutions from which the best resources may be chosen. Each page is a separate entity that can be used as required in a particular situation. There are three kinds of pages (narrative, worksheet, and model) that can be used together as a unit. These pages may be used as presented or adopted for in-service and pre-service workshops. *Providing Programs for Gifted and Talented* is a handbook that explains, illustrates, and applies information.

Programs, Leaders, Consultants, and Other Resources In Gifted and Talented Education, Karnes, Francis and Peddicord, Herschel (1980). Charles C. Thomas. 301–327 East Lawrence Avenue, Springfield, IL 62703

School and parent groups that want to initiate, develop, or evaluate local gifted and talented programs often need the assistance of national organizations, local and state consultants, and other resources. *Programs, Leaders, Consultants, and Other Resources in Gifted and Talented Education* offers descriptions of gifted and talented preschool, elementary, and secondary programs including visual and performing arts programs from throughout the United States.

The names, addresses, professional backgrounds, and contributions of over forty national leaders in gifted and talented education are provided. The same kind of information is cited for state consultants who can provide a wide range of services in the development and support of programs for gifted and talented students. There also is a listing, by states, of various persons who represent possible consultant services to gifted and talented education programs. The last section of this book describes a wide range of other resources including sources of funding, support organizations, periodicals, teacher training institutions, and alternative schools and programs. This book was published in 1980 and therefore some of the information presented may need to be updated.

Educational Psychology of the Gifted, Khatena, Joe (1982). John Wiley and Sons, 605 Third Avenue, New York, NY 10016

One of the recent books about identifying and providing services for gifted and talented students is *Educational Psychology of the Gifted,* by Joe Khatena. The author's long association with E. Paul Torrance flavors the book with sensitivity to creativity as a major issue in education of gifted and talented students. Unlike many texts about gifted and talented students that emphasize academic and intellectual giftedness, this book also contains much information about students who are talented in the visual and performing arts.

Khatena's book is an excellent introduction to, and survey of, historical and current writings about psychology of the gifted. Among the topics discussed are history, definition, identification, creativity, intelligence, teaching guidance, special groups, school provisions, and support systems relative to gifted and talented students including students who are talented in the arts. The book contains many graphs and diagrams that provide visual integration of the topics discussed. We found these to be easily understood; visually oriented readers will appreciate them.

Reaching for the Stars: 7 Using Knowledge about Creativity with the Gifted/ Talented, Mallis, Jackie and Heinemann, Alison. (1979). **Reaching for the Stars: 8 Providing Enrichment Activities for the Gifted/Talented,** Mallis, Jackie and Gilman, Sharlene (1979). Multi-Media Arts, Box 14486, Austin, TX 78716

Multi Media Arts, in Austin, Texas, offers a number of resources for group leaders of workshops for teachers of gifted and talented students. Ten *Reaching for the Stars* workbooks constitute a mini-course to be used to educate such teachers. Each workbook deals with a particular topic and includes a statement of goals and objectives, a brief rationale, a user's preassessment, an assortment of learning activities, a post assessment, suggested resources, a bibliography, and a list of additional readings. Of special interest to art educators are #7, *Using Knowledge About Creativity With the Gifted/Talented* and #8, *Providing Enrichment Activities For the Gifted and Talented.* These workbooks were pilot tested with sixty professionals and later field tested with participants in a number of school districts.

The Creativity workbook provides activities to measure creativity, encourage divergent thinking, and promote brainstorming and productive thinking. Guilford's Structure of the Intellect model is presented in the first part of the Creativity workbook. Activities related to Guilford's model are presented to acquaint teachers with his theory. In the second part of this workbook, tasks related to definition of creativity, how to introduce creative activities in the classroom, examples of creative writing by gifted students, and essays by a number of experts about methods for teaching creative activities are presented.

The Enrichment Activities workbook uses Renzulli's Enrichment Triad Model to organize science, mathematics, arts, music, and literature activities for enrichment learning and to explore student interests and encourage critical thinking using a variety of approaches. Piaget's Theory of Child Development and Bloom and Krathwohl's Taxonomy of Educational Objectives are included as organizers of other activities in this workbook. Enrichment is defined, specific examples are given, and enrichment activities are presented. A large portion of the workbook is devoted to reproductions of articles from which teachers can derive educational content.

Sampler Kits are offered in conjunction with each of the *Reaching for the Stars* work-texts. These Sampler Kits include books, records, games, and kits offered by other publishers. The contents of each Sampler Kit are referenced as learning materials appropriate to activities in each *Reaching for the Stars* workbook.

Both workbooks are valuable resources for anyone conducting inservice education for teachers of gifted and talented students. Art teachers will have to adapt these workbooks to their needs. In a few reproductions of articles, the quality of printing is poor and difficult to read. These two workbooks offer valuable bibliographies of both printed material and other resources such as films, kits, and other teaching resources.

Guiding the Gifted Child: A Practical Source For Parents and Teachers, Webb, James T., Meckstroth, Elizabeth A., and Tolan, Stephanie S. (1982). Ohio Psychological Publishing Company, 5 East Long Street. Suite 610, Columbus, OH 43215

Guiding the Gifted Child deals with emotional problems confronting bright, talented youngsters and support systems they need from parents and teachers to survive and flourish. This book includes five sections that focus on problems commonly experienced by gifted children and others in their families, such as sibling relations, peer relations, motivation, discipline, depression, and breaking with tradition.

The first section gives an overview of giftedness along with underlying myths and stereotypes that exist about gifted children. Steps are suggested to encourage self-esteem, self-respect, and self-identity. The second section focuses more specifically on characteristics, frequently occuring problems, and particular suggestions for modifying behavior. The third section consists of an open letter, by the mother of an exceptionally gifted child, to parents and teachers of gifted children. An annotated bibliography of recommended resources for increasing understanding and developing skills in guiding gifted children comprises the forth section. In the final section, a list of organizations that work with parents of gifted children is presented.

According to the authors, when gifted and enrichment classes do not exist, or where they may be curtailed due to fiscal cut-backs or other factors within the school system, programs for nuturing parent techniques become particularly crucial. *Guiding the Gifted Child* is a sourcebook, written in a down-to-earth manner, designed to help parents and teachers understand gifted children and guide them to becoming healthy and contributing members of society.

The Identi-Form System for Gifted Programs: Identification, Assessment, and Beyond, Weber, Patricia and Battaglia, Catherine (1982). Domains of Knowledge, 71 Radcliffe Road, Buffalo, NY 14214

Prepared guidelines that direct identification and screening decisions about gifted and talented students are not readily available. A new *Identi-Form* system for identifying and screening gifted and talented students uses a basic matrix form that has been proven effective for examining many relevant aspects of giftedness and talent. The Identi-Form is used to record tests, performance, and anecdotal data. Test data includes IQ, achievement, creativity, and self-concept measures. Performance data includes academic and creative performance as well as personal aspects such as past performance and productivity. Anecdotal data are based upon such procedures as interviews, peer nomination, and aptitude inventories. These are examined to help screen candidates for inclusion or exclusion in gifted and talented education programs.

Instructions for coding the Identi-Form and formula for weighing the factors recorded and for interpretation of results are contained in this book. Various interactions of above average abilities, task commitment, and creativity are examined to facilitate accurate identification and appropriate selection of students for a gifted and talented education program.

The book explains the process of data collection and recording of data on the *Identi-Form*. Each source of data is explained and justified as an identification procedure. Many examples and samples are provided of traditional and non-traditional identification measures. A number of pages are devoted to explaining how to read the *Identi-Form* categories and interpret their interactions for accurate identification among diverse candidates.

Although categories of art, music, and other are included as components of creative performance, this book fails to establish criteria and standards for judging performance in the arts. It is suggested in the book that teachers create their own criteria for determining superior abilities. This method of assessing creative performance remains therefore idiosyncratic and subjective.

Books and Periodicals
About Teaching Artistically Talented Students

Art Enrichment: How to Implement a Museum/School Program, 1980. Education Office, The Archer M. Huntington Art Gallery, The University of Texas at Austin, Austin, TX 78712

The education staff of the Archer H. Huntington Art Gallery, Austin, Texas, and the Austin Independent School District have worked together to provide an arts enrichment program for gifted and talented elementary students in Austin Schools. Justification of this program is based upon the assumption that many children make few visits to a museum or attempt to see all the exhibitions on display. Few children view special exhibitions or use the museum as an integral part of their learning. The use of museums, however, as educational resources, provides students with learning experiences that cannot be duplicated in classrooms. These kinds of experiences require repeated museum visits, well considered lessons, and stimulating instructors.

Following guidelines used by the Austin Schools, gifted and talented students were selected for a series of museum visits accompanied by in-school learning experiences before and after their visits. The resulting program was a year-long series of interactions with monthly museum visits and carefully structured preparation and follow-up experiences.

The Education Office of the Archer M. Huntington Art Gallery prepared an illustrated booklet, *Art Enrichment: How to Implement a Museum/School Program,* that includes a rationale for such programs and descriptions of how to organize and staff the programs, how to select students, and how to design and evaluate program experiences. Sample forms for identifying students, administering and scoring a drawing test, and evaluating experiences, as well as detailed sample pre-visit, tour, and follow-up lessons are included. There is also a useful bibliography relative to art teaching, museum/school program planning, and program evaluation.

The museum/school art enrichment program is guided by concepts and resources in the museum's exhibitions. Students are always introduced to the exhibition they will visit by *preparation* materials that enable art teachers to get students involved in the exhibit. Each *museum visit* enables students to look at and talk about works of art and to compare works of art with others. At times, students interact with artists, at the museum, or others who demonstrate methods of art making. *Follow-up lessons* are used to reinforce concepts introduced in the preparation and museum visits and include studio activities. This art enrichment program is not product oriented; it is concerned that students understand major ideas and techniques as these relate to the world of art.

This publication is a valuable resource for anyone who wishes to initiate a similar museum program. The step-by-step discussion from initial planning to finalizing a program calendar is easy to follow and practical in terms of implementation. Samples of identification and selection as well as program evaluation forms can be adapted readily to other museum situations. Lesson plan samples are detailed and practical. The book is attractively designed and illustrated and the large print makes it easy to read.

National Directory: Programs for K–12 Artistically Gifted Talented Students, Bachtel-Nash, Ann (1984). Tam's Books Incorporated, 14932 Garfield Avenue, Paramount, CA 90723

This *National Directory of Programs for Artistically Talented Students* is a valuably needed resource that long has been absent from the field. Information in the directory comes from a survey conducted in 1983 and updated in 1984. Every state was contacted and suggested programs were sent questionnaires. Those not responding were contacted a second time. Bachel-Nash explains that some programs are not included because they were not identified or did not respond to the questionnaire in time for publication.

The directory is alphabetized by state; within each state entry programs are alphabetized by title. Each program entry contains a title, categorization (such as summer program, pull-out program, or private school), description (including program design, selection, and arts curricula), financial arrangements, available information materials, and contact person. There is an index with two listings, by program title and by state.

Bachtel-Nash anticipates writing an expanded edition of this directory; this is good news because directories of this kind quickly become outdated. This first effort at gathering information about programs for artistically talented students is admirable and is a practical resource that is quickly becoming dog-eared in our library.

Educating Artistically Talented Students, Clark, Gilbert A. and Zimmerman, Enid (1984). Syracuse University Press, 1600 Jamesville Avenue, Syracuse, NY 13244

"Robert Frost's well known poem, The Road Not Taken (1915), about the differences that can be made in a person's life if he or she takes a less traveled road, is an apt metaphor for educating artistically talented students....A basic premise of this text is that artistically talented students are a unique school population that deserves opportunities to take optional routes that will make a difference, not only to themselves, but to society." (p. 165)

The above excerpt summarizes the philosophy in *Educating Artistically Talented Students*. Contents of this book are based upon five years of research and in-service application. Philosophy and goals are derived from analyses of problems and recommendations are offered about identification, characteristics of students, approaches to teaching, curriculum content and organization, and appropriate administrative settings. There are five chapters in which each of these major topics is discussed. Each chapter begins with a summary of historical research that provides a background for discussion and recommendations based upon analyses of current practices in the education of artistically talented students.

In the first chapter, a background for understanding gifted and talented education is discussed and a program structure for artistically talented students is set forth. Chapter two presents an extended list of student characteristics derived from historical research and a discussion of identification procedures currently used and recommendations for effective identification practices. Past teacher characteristics and teaching strategies are reviewed, current practices are analyzed, and recommendations for teacher selection and in-service teacher preparation are made in chapter three.

Chapter four contains a review of past and present curriculum practices and program recommendations for students with superior abilities in the visual arts. A curriculum model for learning experiences in the visual arts is used to suggest organization of sequential art programs for artistically talented students. From past practices used in education of gifted students and a review of contemporary programs for artistically talented students, recommendations for effective administrative arrangements are made in chapter five. In the final chapter, contemporary issues of philosophy and goals, identification, teaching, curriculum content, and administrative arrangements and settings for talented art students are discussed.

The following excerpt is from a review by Karen Rogers that appeared in *Roeper Review*, 1985, 7 (4), 264–65.

"Educating Artistically Talented Students is written in a clear, simple-to-read style. It is well organized with each section of every chapter summarized. The book has many black and white illustrations of student art work, classroom scenes, or museum interior photographs appropriately placed within the text. Although the book is intended primarily for elementary and secondary classroom teachers and art instructors, it will also prove of value to school administrators, gifted program coordinators, parents, and others concerned with educating the artistically gifted" (p. 265).

Dissertations About Educating Artistically Talented Students, University Microfilms International, 300 North Zeeb Road, Ann Arbor, MI 48106

During the past decade, a number of researchers have studied and reported various aspects of the characteristics and education of gifted and talented students in the visual arts. The following brief summaries report contents of six dissertations that may be of interest to those involved in educating artistically talented students. Each dissertation is reported by author's name, date, title, abstract number, and a brief description.

Wood, R. L. (1976). An Analysis of Certain Fine Arts High Schools in the United States Including the Alabama School of Fine Arts (77–12, 283). This study was based on a survey of nineteen fine arts high schools in the United States in respect to their organizational, administrative, and curricular practices. The results were then used to assess the Alabama School of Fine Arts.

Clay, V. H. (1978). Education of Artistically Talented Secondary Students as Evidenced by the Pennsylvania Governor's School for the Arts (7902690). Five high schools for students talented in the arts were studied with an emphasis upon describing the Pennsylvania Governor's School of the Arts. These sources were used to determine concepts and strategies appropriate to the education of talented secondary students.

Westfried, I. B. (1978). An Exploratory Study of the Effects of the Pennsylvania Governor's School for the Arts on Self Attitudes and Leadership Activity of Artistically Talented and Creative Adolescents (7905607). In this study, 260 students who attended the Pennsylvania Governor's School of the Arts were administered a battery of tests that measured their self-attitudes and leadership activities as affected by attending a fine arts high school. The positive effects of attending such a high school are reported in relation to pretest, posttest, and follow-up test results.

Fellman, C. R. (1978). Conversations with Child Artists (7817744). Thirty-three interviews with elementary students identified as "child artists" at a public school in Ithaca, New York form the basis of this study. This study does not analyze the interviews but simply reports them as conversations between an art teacher and some of her students.

Chetelet, F. J. (1982). A Preliminary Investigation Into Life Situations and Environments Which Nurture the Artistically Gifted and Talented Child (8305624). The purpose of this study was to identify factors that support early development of art talent. Six artistically talented students, aged eleven to fourteen, were interviewed and their lives compared to the early lives of six eminent artists. The environment and adults in it were shown to have a significant influence on the development of artistic talent.

Loomer, S. C. (1982). A Campus Microcosm: Creativity and Non-Creativity of Gifted Students in Art Settings and Social Situations (8304124). Thirty-six artistically talented high school students at Virginia's Governor's School For the Gifted were studied in a summer arts program. As a participant observer in two fine arts classes and other situations, the researcher studied classroom interactions and student creative behavior. Creative behavior was found to occur more frequently in social situations than in art classes due to the students' conservatism in their art attitudes and taste.

These six studies provide information about model programs and methods for understanding characteristics and behaviors of artistically talented students. Some are useful research models for others interested in designing or evaluating programs for, and increasing our understanding of, artistically talented students. For reprints of these and other dissertations, be sure to include a complete citation, including the abstract number, if requesting a specific reprint.

Identifying Students with Artistic Talent, The Area Agency 7, 3712 Cedar Heights Drive, Cedar Falls, IA

Many face problems of identifying and selecting artistically-talented students for special programs. For many years, educators have suggested using a work-sample technique. This is a technique in which common, standardized experiences are assigned to all participants or applicants and the results are judged comparatively. The primary advantage of the work-sample identification technique is use of shared, standardized tasks.

The Identifying Students With Artistic Talent (ISAT) project in Iowa was an attempt to create an identification device based upon the work-sample technique. The developers wanted to create an identification procedure that could be easily implemented and quickly scored. This project was federally funded and focused upon rural and urban schools where art is taught by classroom teachers.

A booklet and filmstrip, made available in 1981 as a result of this project, serve as identification devices. Standardized tasks, to be used across all grades, include a direct observation drawing, an imaginative drawing, and a three-dimensional project.

Good, average, and poor results at grades two to eight and for high school students are shown as black and white illustrations. The accompanying filmstrip presents the same illustrations as projected images in color. The ISAT booklet also includes a reproducible information sheet for parents, brief lists of student characteristics that can be used in an identification program, and suggestions for implementation of programs for artistically-gifted students.

These materials should be used only as a guide for districts and schools that are attempting to solve the problem of identifying and selecting artistically talented students for special programs. Many of the judgements about good, average and poor art work shown as examples in these materials are questionable. Local, agreed-upon criteria for such choices might be developed from use of these materials.

The Gifted and Talented in Art: A Guide to Program Planning, Hurwitz, Al (1983). Davis Publications, Worcester, MA 01608

The Gifted and Talented in Art is a pioneer work in the area of educational programs for students who are talented in the visual arts. The book is divided into three sections: defining artistic giftedness, planning a program, and model programs. The brief discussion of artistic giftedness covers topics such as when talent begins, relationship of intelligence to artistic giftedness, and characteristics of visually gifted students.

For those planning programs for artistically talented students, initiation, funding, identification, curriculum, location, evaluation, and dissemination are covered in ways designed to help establish such programs. Of special interest is the section about curriculum in which a number of suggested activities, designated as elementary, junior high, and high school levels, are described and illustrated.

Thirteen diverse model programs from throughout the United States are described in terms of their level, funding, identification procedures, program objectives, structure, curriculum, evaluation, and person to contact for further information. These descriptions offer models of the numerous ways in which the needs of artistically talented students are being met in a variety of settings. In an appendix, a number of sample forms are offered. These include evaluation, personal characteristics appraisal, parent notification letters, and student program evaluation forms that can be duplicated or adapted.

One of the strengths of this book is its numerous illustrations from both the United States and other parts of the world that are examples of art work of talented students at a variety of ages. These illustrations help establish teacher expectations of what can be accomplished by highly talented students. The curriculum examples and forms found in the appendix are valuable resources that should be helpful for program planning. The introductory chapters cover important topics that might have been expanded. The remainder of the book should be useful and easy to adapt to specific programs for students talented in the visual arts.

Gifted and Talented in Art Education, Madeja, Stanley (Ed.) (1983). National Art Education Association, 1916 Association Drive, Reston, VA 22091

This book reports fourteen exemplary art programs offered throughout the country. The programs were identified by a national review process that examined reports of about seventy-five programs and selected the fourteen that are described by program directors.

Each exemplary program report includes program overview, goals, student population, location, and a narrative description of the teaching and course content. In addition, program support, unique features, and program results based upon evaluation and follow-up are presented. Each program report is accompanied by several illustrations.

The book is divided into three sections; the first gives a cross section of instructional programs that are based in schools or communities. The programs reviewed serve students from kindergarten through senior high school in such states as Arkansas, California, Louisiana, New Jersey, and New York. The programs range from a local school's printmaking program to description of a comprehensive arts-magnet high school curriculum. Section two reports programs for artistically talented students that serve a state or national audience, including programs in Indiana, Oklahoma, Georgia, Pennsylvania, and South Carolina. The Arts Recognition and Talent Search program is reported as serving talented students throughout the U.S. Each of these programs has received national recognition and several have a lengthy history of service to artistically talented students. The last section contains commentaries about aspects of programs for gifted and talented students. The first article discusses programs about art for academically gifted students and programs for artistically gifted students. The second article reports a lengthy follow-up study and describes influences of a special program on later school and career choices.

This book offers art teachers with an interest in teaching talented art students a number of models of ways to structure and implement programs. Art teachers interested in communicating with program directors throughout the country who have been successful in providing services to artistically talented students will find a variety of contact possibilities.

Ideas For Teaching Gifted Students: Visual Arts, Mallis, Jackie (Ed.). (1982). Multi-Media Arts, Box 14486, Austin, TX 78716

Ideas For Teaching Gifted Students: Visual Arts is a compilation of art lessons from over twenty sources or authors. The editor has organized them from primary to secondary levels of difficulty although she also has pointed out that "the unit topics are not identified as primary, intermediate, etc., because the range of talents among gifted students varies so much" (p. iii). This is an excellent decision; teachers using materials such as these should diagnose their student's abilities and assign tasks appropriate to challenging the knowledge and skills of their students, regardless of their grade level or age.

This book contains a myriad of lessons or units about such wide-ranging topics as line, marine art, calligraphy, industrial design, making movies without a camera, and art and architecture. Each unit is presented thoroughly enough to allow teachers to use the unit with their students. Many lessons cite resource sources to embellish the unit, such as books, films, filmstrips, etc. Many, though not all, contain an evaluation activity. Black and white illustrations, as line drawings, are used to show how to create something or to exemplify a concept to be taught.

The book was printed by off-set and lacks the graphic or visual quality we often associate with art textbooks. This means, however, that it is considerably less expensive than might otherwise be the case. The quality of the content of the units and lessons varies as does the quality of the writing. Nevertheless, *Ideas For Teaching Gifted Students: Visual Arts* is an invaluable resource for teachers with talented students in the visual arts.

Multi-Media Arts, the publisher, offers a number of publications about teaching gifted and talented students, including its "Reaching For The Stars" series. These include activities related to literature, dance, music, and theater and feature activities designed to develop creativity, problem solving, and independent inquiry by gifted and talented students.

Visual Arts in Gifted Programs: Thirty-One Current Programs Described, Moody, Joseph G. (1983). 4502 Sun Valley SW, Albuquerque, NM 87105

This book is the result of a two-year study about visual arts in gifted programs throughout the United States based on a National ART-TAG survey conducted in 1981 and a detailed summary of thirty-one current visual arts programs for gifted students. In *Visual Arts in Gifted Programs,* programs are described that are based in museums, universities, and arts high schools with an emphasis on public school based programs in individual schools or school districts. Twenty states and the District of Columbia, small rural communities to large metropolitan areas, and grades kindergarten to twelve are represented.

Each of the thirty-one programs is presented in a double-page format, with the same information given for each program. This standard format reflects the survey form, included in the book, that was used to obtain information. The thirty-one programs are described in terms of contact person, levels served, number of personnel, present funding, per student cost, relationship to school program, delivery system, inception date, size, ART-TAG representation, use of a sequential curriculum and theoretical model, courses offered, and identification and evaluation procedures. Described in further detail are selection processes, program summary, evaluation of program effectiveness and student growth, identification and selection of teachers/directors, and publications. An introduction that summarizes information found in the book and a report about the National ART-TAG survey contribute information about the current status of visual arts programs in the United States.

Performing Tree Publications: The Fourth R. Strengthening Your Instructional Program Through the Arts, Artist's Handbook: To Work in Communities, Schools or Social Institutions, Guide to the Performing and Visual Arts, Learning Through Visual Art, Performing Tree, Incorporated, 1320 West Third Street, Los Angeles, CA 90017

Performing Tree is a group of experienced artists and specialists in Los Angeles who have created arts programs designed to increase communication skills, enhance self concepts, and encourage critical thinking for exceptional children, including the gifted and talented. Performing Tree offers workshops, artist-in-residence programs, grant writing assistance, arts performances, consultant services to California schools, and publications and instructional materials that can be used in other parts of the country. Performing Tree is supported by more than sixty individuals, corporations, businesses, and private foundations.

Performing Tree publications are based upon the philosophy of the *Visual and Performing Arts Framework for California Public Schools;* it stresses using Bloom's (et al.) *Taxonomy of Educational Objectives: Cognitive* as a basis for various arts experiences. Comprehensive arts education in which the arts are taught separately and in relation to one another guides Performing Tree's programs.

Artists' Handbook

Performing Tree offers a useful publication, *Artists' Handbook,* that is a manual for artists-in-residence in community agencies, schools, or other social institutions. Artists-in-schools are relatively common throughout the country and often occur in programs for artistically talented students. This handbook offers guidelines to improve the services and educational benefits of such programs. Specific guidelines are given for resumé writing, planning, implementation, publicity and documentation, evaluation, and post-residency follow-up. Actual worksheets, release forms, evaluation forms, and check lists are included. Suggestions for teaching appropriate to various audiences, situations, and circumstances are presented in this handbook.

Guide to the Performing and Visual Arts

Classroom teachers who want to incorporate the arts into their enrichment activities for gifted and talented students would benefit from the *Guide to the Performing and Visual Arts* offered by Performing Tree. The book is divided into two parts. Part one, The Arts, deals with the performing arts of dance, music, and drama and is intended to be used as a supplement to arts performances in schools and communities. It is, however, general enough to be used in any classroom. Part two, The Arts and the Curriculum, deals with integrating basic elements of the arts into the core curriculum of English and mathematics. Visual arts activities are presented frequently in both parts and lists of additional instructional materials, books, and other resources also are included.

Learning Through Visual Art

This publication addresses the elementary classroom teacher and provides many examples of how to use art projects that stress self-awareness and self-expression, integrated with study of language arts, social science, mathematics, and science. Lessons identified by grade levels are related to aesthetic perception, creative expression, art heritage, and aesthetic valuing. Each lesson states a concept, objective, vocabulary, materials, motivation, progression, analysis, and extensions. Paintings in poetry, geometric designs, tree motifs, and a museum in your classroom are a few representative titles. A glossary, selected resources and references, and suggested art reproductions also are included.

In addition to these publications, Performing Tree offers *Learning Through Dance/Movement, Learning Through Mime/Creative Dramatics, Puppets and Learning,* and *The Fourth R.* The puppetry book is a practical guide to puppet making and performance and presents information about puppets from around the world. *The Fourth R* gives information about how to install a comprehensive arts program at all levels of public education.

Performing Tree publications are well organized, easy to use in the classroom, and consistent to a clearly stated philosophy. There are many lessons at different grade levels offered and teachers of students who are talented in the visual arts can select appropriate lessons for group or individual instruction. Care should be exercised when using Performing Tree publications that the integrity of the visual art curriculum is maintained and not lost to comprehensive art objectives.

Project Art Band: A Program for Visually Gifted Children, Education Department, DeCordova Museum, Sandy Point Road, Lincoln, MA 01773

The DeCordova Museum, with funding from the Massachusetts Department of Education, has published an identification, implementation, and curriculum document to help schools and museums create programs for visually talented students. Published in 1982, *Project Art Band: A Program for Visually Gifted Children* is a set of guidelines for the implementation of programs for schools in any part of the country. Adaptable guidelines for staffing, staff training, materials, facilities, and budgeting are offered.

Of particular interest are the identification procedures used by Project Art Band. David Baker, chief consultant, designed the project's primary identification instruments: *The Narrative Drawing Assessment* and *The Visual Memory Assessment*. These instruments proved successful for screening students for this project (see p. 47 for a description of these tests).

The two Baker tests provided alternatives to many tests currently used such as The Torrance Tests of Creativity. The Torrance Tests were found to be expensive and did not contribute to accurate identification of visually talented students. The Baker tests, however, have not been standardized or validated with other populations and their reliability has not been proven.

Included in *Project Art Band* are thirty pages of suggested lessons for visually talented students that are designed to teach criticism skills, problem solving skills, technical skill development, and appreciation of roles of artists in society. These lessons are briefly stated and suggest activities that might be used with artistically talented students, but need much more elaboration in order to be implemented easily.

Mommy, It's A Renoir! Wolf, Aline D. (1984). Parent Child Press, P.O. Box 767, Altoona, PA 16603

This paperback, 8½″ × 11″ book is a resource for parents and teachers of preschool, nursery school, and primary school age children. It is subtitled Art Postcards for Art Appreciation and A Parent and Teacher Handbook. The author, as a mother and teacher, shares many ideas she has developed to help others "who want to experience the delight of introducing beautiful paintings to young children."

All activities in this book are based upon manipulation of postcard size art reproductions. They range from simple matching of identical card images to creating a time line of art. The author claims the activities can begin with children as young as three and that, as they increase in difficulty, are adaptable to children's levels of experience rather than their specific age. They are adaptable, therefore, to the quick learning of artistically talented students as well as to the needs of handicapped and special populations.

There are six steps outlined in the book: matching identical paintings, pairing companion paintings, grouping paintings by one artist, learning the names of artists, learning the names of famous paintings, learning about schools of art, grouping paintings from the same school, and using a time line of art history. Each of these steps is presented at an easiest, intermediate, or advanced level with differing degrees of difficulty.

A general discussion about why and how to use art reproduction postcards is presented in the book's introduction. In Part Three, after the activities are described, there is an important discussion about obtaining, mounting, and storing art reproduction postcards and, more importantly, a generalized discussion of major schools of art history. This is helpful for parents and teachers without a background in the history of art. The author makes it clear that such a background in unnecessary and that learning *with* students is both exciting and rewarding.

The book is profusely illustrated with black and white drawings that explain the text and help others involve children in the activities described. Sets of pre-arranged postcard size reproductions, to be used with the steps outlined in the text, are obtainable from the publisher. Teachers need not be limited to these sets, however, and could adapt the tasks outlined to any particular set of postcard reproductions.

Books With Background Information

The Artist, Feldman, Edmund B. (1982). Prentice Hall, Englewood Cliffs, NJ 67362

Many gifted art students have misconceptions about the role of the artist in society. The artist is usually viewed either as a Bohemian starving in a garret or as a famous popular celebrity. In this book, *The Artist*, Feldman describes twenty or more artist's roles that de-mystify the role of the artist in society. For talented junior and senior high school art students and their teachers, reading this book can increase their awareness and understanding of the past and present roles of the artist in society.

The book begins with cave painting and ends with contemporary concerns such as the woman artist, black artist, and ethnic artist. Feldman introduces the reader to great numbers of artist's roles and motivations. He surveys historical, social, economic, personal, and psychological reasons people have made art for several centuries.

Students at all levels, just as most adults, carry many false stereotypes about artists; Feldman certainly calls to question such misunderstandings. He explains why there is an artist mystique and why there should not be. His descriptions of the Bohemian Artist (Chapter 8) and the Gallery Idol (Chapter 11) are delightful to read. They set aside, with some degree of ironic scolding, the "dandified aristocrat" who aspires to being called artist and the galleries and dealers who operate "art boutiques" where "art styles are force-fed or hothouse grown, prematurely buried or arbitrarily resurrected" and "lose their significance as vehicles of serious artistic ideas and insights" (p. 199). These two models are countered by the Illustrator (Chapter 9) and the Industrial Designer (Chapter 10) as non-bohemian, contract artists whose careers parallel those of the Classical Artisan (Chapter 4) or the Medieval Guildsman (Chapter 5). In the last chapter, The Hyphenated Artist, Feldman discusses artist-teacher, woman-artist, ethnic-artist, etc. and provides a discussion of contemporary problems.

The Artist contains 184 images that illustrate the text. Illustration captions are often seventy-five to one hundred words and, in themselves, are reason enough to read The Artist; they succinctly present many of the major issues that are in the book. The text that surrounds the illustrations is a further reward.

This book is recommended to high school students preparing or thinking of preparing for an art career. Some of Feldman's ideas are controversial and teachers should read the book before they recommend it to young readers. In many cases, teacher's interpretations and explanations will help young readers understand some of Feldman's broadly drawn conclusions about the artist in society.

My Name is Asher Lev, Potok, Chaim (1972). Fawcett Book Company, 1515 Broadway, New York, NY 10036 (paperback); Alfred A. Knopf, 201 East 50th Street, New York, NY 10022 (hardback)

My Name is Asher Lev, by Chaim Potok, is a popular book that was on the New York Times Best Seller List for six months. Asher Lev, the book's hero, is an extraordinarily talented artist who, ultimately, rejects his family and his faith in his struggle to reach maturity as an artist. This compelling book traces Asher Lev's life through his early childhood and school years while he becomes aware of, and develops, his artistic talent.

The book would be of value to all art teachers and parents who are interested in understanding the development of a young person's maturation as an artist. Many art programs use intensity of interest and desire to make art an entrance criterion that distinguishes students with superior potential in the arts. My Name is Asher Lev is clearly a record of a young person's sacrifices that are motivated by his unquenchable need to create art. The record of his first crayon drawings to his fully mature paintings is a record of dispute and isolation from people who do not understand his overwhelming need to create drawings and paintings.

In Potok's works, "Not only should the artist be intoxicated with the thing he wants to express" but he should find a "kindred spirit" with whom to study. Unlike many young artists, Asher Lev is fortunate to find his own kindred spirit in Jacob Kahn, an artist who becomes Lev's teacher-mentor. Kahn guides Asher Lev through his troubled adolescence and early adulthood, teaching the skills and techniques that Lev needs as well as developing his intuitive qualities of artistic imagination. All persons who work with highly talented young people should read this moving and sensitive story as a background to understanding the joys and anguish that accompany the development of superior art talents.

Art from Many Hands, Schuman, Jo Miles (1981). Davis Publications, 50 Portland Street, Worcester, MA 01608

Global education challenges educators to develop programs that reflect such matters as the unity and diversity of peoples throughout the world and the need for international cooperation in shaping the future. Many talented art students who become leaders in the visual arts will need to develop knowledge, skills, and values to live effectively in a world that is characterized by "ethnic diversity, cultural pluralism, and increasing interdependence" of nations (National Council for Social Studies, 1981).

Art from Many Hands can serve as a sourcebook for finding a variety of multicultural art projects based on the crafts of West Africa, the Middle East, Europe, Asia, Mexico, Central America, South America, Caribbean Islands, the United States, and Canada. In this book, art from a particular region, such as adinkra cloth from Ghana, is presented as one of several textile arts from Africa. Illustrations of adinkra cloth, adinkra stamps carved from calabashes, and adinkra symbols are used as a basis for discussion. For each project presented, traditional materials and materials that can be adapted for classroom use are suggested. For example, adinkra stamps are traditionally carved from calabashes and printed with black dye; potato stamps and acrylic paint, for your children, and linoleum and printer's ink for older children, are substituted for traditional materials. Step-by-step instructions with illustrations of children doing art projects also are included. The appendix contains on extensive annotated bibliography that is related to the book's content. *Art from Many Hands* contains full color and black and white illustrations ranging from clay birds from Mexico to Chinese calligraphy. There are many drawings of symbols from a variety of cultures.

This book emphasizes basic craft techniques from all over the world. Art teachers should include art concepts found in art making, art history, art criticism, and aesthetics, as well as an interdisciplinary approach, in lessons based on resources found in this book. For example, a lesson about adinkra cloth also could include concepts about symbols, patterns, positive and negative space, the history of textile design in Africa, comparison of adinkra cloth with contemporary mass-produced textile designs, and discussion about why adinkra cloth is exhibited in museums.

Talented art students should be encouraged to use craft sources in the book as a beginning point after which they should conduct research to learn about a particular culture and symbols and techniques used in the culture and then create an art work that is adapted, not copied, from the art work found within particular cultures. Teachers also should use painting, drawing, sculpture, and other works of art found in a variety of cultures to supplement the emphasis on craft objects found in the book so that a unity between fine art and craft is achieved.

Teaching Children to Draw: A Guide for Teachers and Parents, Wilson, Marjorie and Wilson, Brent (1982). Prentice Hall, Englewood Cliffs, NJ 07632

Majorie Wilson and Brent Wilson have studied, during the last decade, many young artists in the United States and abroad. Their book, *Teaching Children to Draw: A Guide for Teachers and Parents,* reports many of these studies and draws generalizations about common concerns and traits of young artists. An important contribution of this book is its focus upon individualized instruction and guidance and the nurturance of children's spontaneous art.

Many parents of artistically talented children wonder how they can help such talent develop and flourish. The Wilsons offer sample dialogues and drawing activities that help young people increase their drawing vocabulary, imagination, and abilities to tell stories with drawings. The suggested activities and sample dialogues are based upon one-to-one or small group interactions. They are most appropriate for non-school environments and stress spontaneous drawing in the child's home environment.

The Wilsons offer unique insights into why children draw and why their drawings look the way they do. They also discuss cultural influences on children's graphic development that help explain the appearance of various kinds of drawings. The authors draw upon their years of interviews and study of children who make spontaneous drawings to share insights about how children learn to draw. The authors discuss artistically gifted children only briefly, though the myriad of illustrations and case histories are a record of the graphic development of many artistically-talented children.

Parents and teachers working with young people are offered much guidance about how to influence a child's development in drawings and trigger imaginative and spontaneous graphic art. From encouraging copying to playing such games as The Jelly Bean Factory, parents and others are offered many suggestions and explanations that can nurture young people's drawing abilities. It is an excellent resource book for anyone teaching drawing to gifted and talented students.

This book is profusely illustrated, but the illustrations sometimes interfere with the text. Because the type face of the captions and text are the same, it is often difficult to know where one ends and the other begins.

Catalogs, Guides, And Media Services

Arts Alive, Agency for International Technology, Box A, Bloomington, IN 47401

Arts Alive is a video series of thirteen programs to help students understand, appreciate, and respond to the arts. Included are four art forms: visual art, dance, music, and drama. Eight of the programs cover elements and principles of the four art forms and the remaining four programs address these art forms together. Programs stress that art can be found everywhere, that personal experience, intent, and technological innovation all affect an artist's work and that the arts play an important role in a variety of jobs.

The programs combine dramatic and documentary formats. The dramatic segments show students in realistic school settings as they encounter and become involved in the arts, whereas the documentary segments show professional artists talking about and making their art.

Arts Alive was developed for use by both non-arts teachers and art specialists. Programs are structured so that knowing about the arts is given as much emphasis as participating in the arts. In most programs, art history, art criticism, and aesthetics are integral parts in addition to sections that show students and arts professionals making and performing in the arts.

A teacher's guide that accompanies the series provides instructional information and follow-up activities. Each lesson consists of four parts: an introductory section that includes Key Terms related to the program content, a Before the Program Section to help orient students to the program topic, a Program Summary, and After the Program discussion questions and activities.

This instructional series has won several awards for its excellent content and attractive production. Students and artists who appear in the series provide role models for artistically talented students. The Elements of the Visual Arts, Creating the Visual Arts, Arts and Self Expression, Arts and Social Messages, Arts and Technology, and Arts and Work are programs especially relevant for students talented in the visual arts.

National Public Radio Cassette Catalogue, National Public Radio, 2025 M Street, NW, Washington, DC 20036

In this day of blockbuster science fiction films, video-discs, VCRs, and one or two television sets in most homes and classrooms, we sometimes forget that radio also provides exciting entertainment and information. National Public Radio is attempting to renew interest in listening resources with an extensive catalog of tapes based upon previously broadcast radio programs. A great many topics, famous voices, and other oral resources are described and offered to schools and individuals with playback facilities.

Tapes of particular interest for teachers of gifted and talented students include previously broadcasted Options in Education and Voices in the Wind Programs. Voices of gifted and talented children, their teachers and administrators, and broadcast interviewers are heard on these tapes. They are particularly suited for parent-teacher meetings or for in-service teacher workshops and address professional problems of providing school programs for gifted and talented students. Many other tapes about education, the arts, and special education in the National Public Radio catalog are suitable for direct use in the classroom as motivation or enrichment materials for students. These tapes are technically superior and the conversations are lively and interesting. For workshop use, visual materials could be used to augment the oral presentations on the tapes.

Metropolitan Museum of Art, Subscription Service, 225 Gracie Station, New York, NY 10161

The Metropolitan Museum of Art (MET) in New York City offers high quality and unique materials for enrichment of art instruction in schools. Teachers who work with individuals or small groups of artistically talented students will find a wealth of resources available through an inexpensive subscription service offered by the MET. Subscribers receive a bi-monthly newsletter; illustrated theme catalogs with such items as posters, prints, three-dimensional art reproductions, presents for children, greeting cards, and calendars; a quarterly museum bulletin; sale catalogs of books, prints, and reproductions; and reduced admission to the MET. All items listed for sale in the catalogs and art works discussed in the bulletins and newsletters are found in the MET's or other museum collections.

Of special interest to teachers of artistically talented students are the annual Presents for Children catalogs. In the past, this catalog has offered books, games, cards, three-dimensional art reproductions, art materials, and art activity sets. For example, a Hounds and Jackal Game set features sculptured dog-and-jackal-headed pieces that reproduce handsome ivory pieces in the museum's collection. An accompanying booklet describes the history and rules of this ancient Egyptian game. Students can learn the art of lettering with a Spencerian Calligraphy Kit. The kit includes four pen points, a pen holder, India Ink, sheets of calligraphy parchment paper, note cards with envelope, and instruction booklet that offers students opportunities to practice the flowing, ornate style of Spencerian writing. A Young Collector's Packet contains three-dimensional reproductions and a text about each object. Included in this packet are a Chinese coin, an Indian Buddha, Egyptian amulets, and a fish ring from Ceylon.

All these items could be used to trigger art historical inquiry as well as learnings about the art and culture of other countries. Imaginative teachers will find educational uses for most of the objects, materials, and publications offered by the MET.

National Gallery of Art, Department of Extension Programs, National Gallery of Art, Washington, DC 20565

The National Gallery of Art has found a way to make its collection accessible, through slide sets, films, and video cassettes, anywhere in the country. The Extension Program of the National Gallery lends media programs, free of charge, to educational institutions, community groups, and individuals throughout the United States.

There are many talented art students around the country who do not have access to major museum art collections. Teachers of these students often lack visual resources appropriate to their needs. The National Gallery of Art Extension Services provides an inexpensive means of bringing great works of art into classrooms for talented students anywhere in the United States. The quality of these visual resources is superior and students are offered opportunities to see great works of art and hear narrations by famous people.

Each color slide program includes 35mm slides, a printed text, and an audiocassette. Among the thirty-eight color slide programs are *700 Years of Art, Survey of American Painting, Famous Men and Women in Portraits, African Art, Physics and Painting,* and *Fireworks.* American crafts and folk arts are highlighted in slide programs such as *Folk Arts of the Spanish Southwest, Toys, Dolls,* and *Furniture.* A number of slide programs have been designed for classroom use or individual study and contain a variety of enrichment materials such as *The Chinese Past: 6000 Years of Art and Culture* and *Henri Matisse: Paper Cut-Outs.*

Thirty-four 16mm color/sound motion pictures also are available through the National Gallery Extension Service. Films about artists, arts movements, major themes in art, American history seen through art masterpieces, art from many cultures, and creation and analysis of single art works are listed. A number of these films also are available as ¾" color video-cassettes.

It is difficult to know, from reading the catalog descriptions, for what grades materials are intended. Teachers should preview materials before using them in class. These free loan materials must be ordered at least one month in advance. The materials may be kept for five working days. Borrowers are required only to pay fourth class postage when returning programs to the National Gallery of Art.

Slide Buyer's Guide: An International Directory of Slide Sources for Art and Architecture, Cashman, Norine D. and Braunstein, Mark M. (1985). Libraries Unlimited, Inc., P.O. Box 263, Littleton, CO 80160

This is the fifth edition of the *Slide Buyer's Guide*. It is a practical guide designed to assist teachers, researchers, and librarians in identifying the best sources for art and architecture slides in the United States, Canada, and twenty-eight other countries.

Indexed by subject are more than five hundred individuals, companies, museums, and institutions that offer slides of art and architecture for sale, rent, or exchange. Vendors are listed alphabetically within geographic categories. The following information is included, when possible, for all entries: scope of subject coverage, method of creating masters for slide production, method of making copies for sale, identification supplied in catalogs or with slides, prices and business practices, and terms on which slides may be borrowed temporarily. Alternative sources, including distributors and independent vendors, are listed that offer related slides, such as other images included in a museum's collection. The quality of the slides offered, completeness and accuracy of the identifying information, and promptness and fairness in filling orders also are evaluated.

The *Guide* is designed primarily for discriminating, professional buyers. For less experienced buyers, a small number of major vendors are indicated by an asterisk. These vendors can be counted on to produce good quality slides that are adequately identified, use reasonable business practices, and prompt service. The editors do suggest that smaller vendors who offer excellent slides should not be overlooked.

A small slide library should be established over a number of years by teachers of artistically talented students. Slides that can be used both for individual and group instruction are indispensible for visual arts instruction. This *Guide* is a valuable resource for locating and purchasing appropriate art and architecture slides.

Visual Arts Reference and Research Guide for Artists, Educators, Curators, Historians, and Therapists, Sacca, Elizabeth J. and Singer, Loren R. (1983). Perspecto Press, Visual Arts 204, Concordia University, 1455 de Maisonneuve Blvd. West, Montreal, Quebec H3G 1M8, Canada

How many times have you or your students wanted an answer to a question but not known where to find it? This art reference and research guide was written specifically to help teachers and students, as well as arts professionals, locate source materials in a myriad of subject areas as they relate to the visual arts. In the words of the authors, "The purpose of this guide is to reduce methodological difficulty. It grows out of the authors' conviction that . . . what is needed is a means of gaining access to relevant ideas in related fields" (p. 2).

Reproductions of art works can be used as valuable resources for educating artistically talented students. This acrylic painting is an interpretive value study of a Cézanne painting by a ninth-grade student in the IU Summer Arts Institute. Photo by Loret Falkner.

The guide begins with a Topic Index that provides users with a cross-index system to over two hundred art related topics, twenty-four categories of sources, and 658 annotated descriptions. Numbers are used in the Topic Index that refer users to specific sources about their subject of interest. The extensive list of topics includes sub-references to other topics of related interest, thus extending the utility of the Topic Index.

Reference tools are described in categories that include encyclopedias and dictionaries, biographical sources, bibliographies, periodicals, government publications (from UNESCO, the U.S., Canada, Great Britain, and local sources), almanacs, and audio-visual resources including computer software. These and other categories can be used by teachers and students to locate sources of information about topics being researched. The information sources are very extensive and go well beyond typical or commonly used tools such as encyclopedias.

The topic *gifted children*, for example, is cross-indexed to two subject bibliographies, numbers 225 and 309. These numbers are located easily in the *Reference and Research Guide* in which listings are found in numerical order. Research tool #225 is: Anthony, J. B. and Anthony, Margaret M. *The Gifted and Talented: A Bibliography and Resource Guide*. Pittsfield, MA: Berkshire Community, 1981. Research tool #309 is: Laubenfels, Jean. *The Gifted Student: An Annotated Bibliography*. Wesport, CO: Greenwood, 1977. Although these are the only two reference tools cross-listed under *gifted children*, there are numerous other art-related topics that would be useful for teachers of students who are talented in the visual arts.

CREATING TEACHER-MADE INSTRUCTIONAL MATERIALS

Teachers of students who are talented in the visual arts are confronted with the need to provide individualized learning tasks for students who complete class art projects sooner than others. At other times, teachers may wish to use art related tasks that are independent of studio projects, as group motivators for looking at and talking about art.

We have devised a number of art tasks based upon the use of small sized art reproductions. They vary in difficulty, complexity, nature of task, time required to complete the task, and use by small groups or individuals. Following are descriptions of various art task activities that we have designed and found useful for teaching artistically talented students at various levels:

Puzzles: Educating visual sensitivity to works of art

1. Obtain two identical art postcard images. Leave one postcard intact and cut the other into ¼″ vertical strips. Place these in an envelope and write instructions for students to place the cut strips over the intact image in correct order.

2. Start with two identical postcard images. Leave one intact and cut key features of the other into small shapes. Place pieces in an envelope and write instructions for students to place the cut pieces in correct positions on the background image.

3. Use two pairs of postcards with images that are similar. Keep one of the pair of postcards intact and cut the other into 1/4″ strips. Place the two postcards and strips in an envelope and write directions to place the cut strips over the two intact images in correct order.

4. A more difficult task would involve cutting two postcards with similar images into strips or squares and having students reconstruct the images without intact postcards to guide the activity.

Contrasting and Comparing Images: Perceiving similarities and differences in works of art

1. Find postcards with similar subject matter and dissimilar styles. Students can contrast and compare differences and similarities in the works of art, either individually or in small groups, and write these down for further discussion.

2. The above tasks can be graded in difficulty by having less and less obvious differences between the paired images until the students are able to discuss similarities and differences in images that are very similar in both style and content.

Sorting Images: Discerning content and style differences in works of art

1. Gather about two dozen images that fall into four easily discernable groups according to subject matter (four portraits, landscapes, still-lifes, abstracts, etc.). Package these in an envelope and have small groups of students

sort these into categories and discuss why they formed their groupings.

2. Obtain about two dozen images of the same subject matter created in two or three different styles. Students then can group these images according to style, subtle content, or other differences suggested by the images, such as chronology, color scheme, and mood.

3. Have several groups do sorting tasks. Then ask the groups to move around to view the sortings done by other groups and determine the criteria, through discussion, used by each group.

Art and Non-Art: Discussing and defining art

1. From diverse sources, collect images of objects in groupings such as architecture, manufactured objects (jewelery, appliances, etc.), handicrafts, photographs, costume design, graphic design (logos, etc.), fabrics, coins, prints, and paintings from a variety of cultures. Make three or four sets of images, in various categories, by mounting twelve to twenty images on $3'' \times 5''$ unlined index cards with rubber cement. Each set should contain one or more qualitatively good images from each category and the images used from various categories should be similar to one another. Images of quilts, Kachina dolls, earrings, or cartoons in each set, for example, should be represented by the same, or a very similar image, in the other sets.

Small groups of students should be given sets of cards and asked to put these cards into two groups; one containing art objects (Art group) and one containing objects that are not classified as art (Non-Art group). The students must agree about which images should be placed in the Art and Non-Art categories. After sorting is completed, students are asked which objects they placed in each category and to give reasons for their placements.

This task is designed to help students think about art and the definition of an art object. The outcome of the discussion is to make students aware that art can be defined in broad open-ended terms and include all major means of visual communication. After discussion, students should understand that all images of objects on the cards could be placed in the Art category.

2. These sets of images can be used in many other ways. When groups of students in the class each have a set of cards, the teacher can ask students to hold up a card that contains an image in response to questions such as: Display an image and ask, Who can find an image similar to this one? Which is the oldest object in your set? Which is the newest? Which is an object not made in the United States? Who can show me an image that is Oriental, African, American, Mexican, etc.? Who has an object made of glass, clay, metal, etc.? Display an image and ask, Who has an image with similar colors to this one? Which image has geometric shapes? Which image is frightening, etc.? Each choice displayed should be defended by discussing the attributes used to answer each question.

3. Individual images should be identified by listing titles, artist, etc. on a card in each set. Students can be asked to do research to learn more about individual images that interest them. Research reports can be delivered to the class and reports about the same, or similar images, can be composed.

Similar tasks can be created inexpensively by teachers appropriate to needs of students in their classes and schools in which they teach. Visuals can be obtained by writing to museums, art publishing companies, and art postcard distributers to obtain postcards, catalogs, and other inexpensive sources of imagery. Multiple copies are useful when creating matched sets of educational materials; try to obtain more than one copy of the images you wish to use in designing inexpensive art tasks.

RESOURCE SOURCE LIST
OF ART-RELATED CATALOGS AND MATERIALS

The following is a representative list of visual arts teaching resource sources, familiar to us, that offer catalogs from which to order art related materials. No claim is made for the completeness of this listing. Catalogs should be requested on school or other official stationery to help ensure prompt delivery of materials. Next to each resource source listed are abbreviations indicating specific materials available. The abbreviations used are:

Filmstrips (Fs)
Fine Art Originals (Fao)
Fine Art Reproductions 2D (F2d)
Fine Art Reproductions 3D (F3d)
Games (G)
Illustrated Art calendars (Ic)
Multimedia Kits (MK)
Museum Catalogs (MC)
Photography (Ph)
Postage Stamps (Ps)
Postcards (Pc)
Posters (Po)
Slides (S)
Small Study Prints (SSP)

Harry N. Abrams, Inc.   F2d, SSP
110 East 59th St.
New York, NY 10022

African Studies Center   Fs, F2d, MK,
University of California   African, Afro-American
Los Angeles, CA 90024   materials

Aiko's Art Materials Import
714 North Wabash Ave.
Chicago, IL 60611

Japanese art materials
and papers

Albright-Knox Art Gallery
1285 Elmwood Ave.
Buffalo, NY 14222

MC, S,
Contemporary artists'
imagery

American Crafts Council
44 W. 53rd Street
New York, NY 10019

Fs, Ph, S of crafts
objects

American Heritage Publishing Company, Inc.
P.O. Box 1776
Marion, OH 43302

F2d, F3d, S,
American historical
replicas

Argus Communications
7440 Natchez Ave.
Niles, IL 60648

Fs, Po,
Study prints-graded
sets

Art Council Aids
P.O. Box 641
Beverly Hills, CA 90210

Fs, S

Art Education, Inc.
28 E. Erie Street
Blauvelt, NY 10913

F2d, Pc, Po,
Multi-Visuals, Poster
sets

Artex Prints, Inc.
200 Temberwick Road
Greenwich, CT 06830

F2d, SSP

Art Extension Press
Box 389
Westport, CT 06880

F2d, SSP

Art Institute of Chicago
Michigan and Adams
Chicago, IL 60603

MC, Pc, S,
Booklets

The Art Museum
Princeton University
Princeton, NY 08540

MC, S

Arts In Society
University of Wisconsin-Extension
610 Langdon Street
Madison, WI 53706

MK,
Thematic kits with
cassettes and slides

Aaron Ashley, Inc.
174 Buena Vista Ave.
Yonkers, NY 10701

F2d

Asian Art Museum of San Francisco Golden Gate Park San Francisco, CA 94118	MC, S Oriental Art imagery
Association of Educational Communications & Technology 1201 Sixteenth Street, N.W. Washington, DC 20036	Fs, MK, F2d, Pc, Visual communication materials
Bellerophon Books 36 Anacapa Santa Barbara, CA 93101	Coloring Books, cultural-historical imagery
The Brooklyn Museum Gallery Shop Eastern Parkway Brooklyn, NY 11238	MC, S
Bowmar Publishers P.O. Box 5225 Glendale, CA 91201	Fs, MK, S
Cahill and Company 145 Palisade Street Dobbs Ferry, NY 10522	Po, IC, F2d, F3d
Cathay House P.O. Box 2064 Falls Church, VA 22042	F2d, F3d, Chinese tomb rubbings
The Center For Humanities, Inc. Two Holland Avenue White Plains, NY 10603	Fs, S, MK, Record, cassette, slide, booklet kits
Cincinnati Art Museum Eden Park Cincinnati, OH 45202	MC, S
The Cleveland Museum of Art 11150 East Boulevard Cleveland, OH 44106	Po, F2d, S
Collector's Guild, Ltd. 185 Madison Avenue New York, NY 10016	Fao, Original art work (prints)
Contemporary Crafts, Inc. 5271 West Pico Blvd. Los Angeles, CA 90019	Fs, S of crafts objects
Creative Playthings, Inc. P.O. Box 1100 Princeton, NJ 08540	G, Pc, Games, cards, color paddles

Davis Publications, Inc.
1E–971 Printers Bldg.
Worcester, MA 01608

Folios of student
work

Donald Art Company, Inc.
90 South Ridge Street
Port Chester, NY 10674

F2d, SSP

Dover Publications
130 Varick Street
New York, NY 10014

F2d, Ph,
Copyright-free imagery in
Pictorial Archive series

Edmund Scientific Company
101 East Gluester Pike
Barrington, NJ 08007

Equipment and materials
for experiential activities

Ethnic American Art Slide Library
College of Arts and Sciences
University of South Alabama
Mobile, AL 36688

S

Educational Dimensions Corporation
P.O. Box 126
Stamford, CT 06904

Fs, MK,
Slide, tape, booklet kits

Environmental Communications
64 Windward Avenue
Venice, CA 90291

Fs, MK, Ph, S

Frederick Douglass Institute
Museum of African Art
316–318 A Street NE
Washington, DC 20002

Fs, F2d, MK,
African, Afro-American
imagery

Fine Arts Philatelists
M.E.D. Sonderegger
P.O. Box 1606
Midland, MI 46840

Ps, Pc,
Fine Arts imagery on
postage stamps

Fine Arts Publications
1346 Chapel Street
New Haven, CT 06511

MK,
Thematic art kits

Fogg Art Museum
Harvard University
Cambridge, MA 02138

MC, S

Frick Collection
1 East 70th Street
New York, NY 10021

MC, S

The Green Tiger Press 7458 Fifth Avenue San Diego, CA 92103	F2d, Romantic illustrators: Potter, Rackham, Wyeth, Pyle . . .
The Solomon R. Guggenheim Museum 1071 Fifth Avenue New York, NY 10028	MC, S
Hirshhorn Museum & Sculpture Garden Museum Shop Smithsonian Institution Washington, DC 20560	MC, S
Hunt Manufacturing Company 1405 Locust Street Philadelphia, PA 19102	Po, S, Lettering, printmaking images, and supplies
Huntington Library and Art Gallery 1151 Oxford Road San Marino, CA 91108	MC, S
International Exhibitions Foundation Editors Building, Suite 310 1729 H. Street, Northwest Washington, DC 20006	MC, catalogs & posters
Arthur Jaffé, Inc. 42 3rd Avenue Mineola, NY 11501	F2d, SSP
Japan Air Lines P.O. Box 777 Burlingame, CA 94010	IC
Krannert Art Museum Gift Shop 500 Peabody Drive University of Illinois Urbana, IL 61801	MC, G, The Design Game
Lambert Studios, Inc. 910 N. La Cienega Boulevard Los Angeles, CA 90069	F2d, SSP
Light Impressions P.O. Box 940 Rochester, NY 14603	Ph, All forms of photographic imagery and publications
Los Angeles County Museum of Art Bookshop 5905 Wilshire Boulevard Los Angeles, CA 90036	MC, S

Longman Incorporated Schools Division 19 W. 44th Street New York, NY 10036	Jackdaws
The Maine Photographic Resource 2 Central Street Rockport, ME 04856	Ph, Po
Media-Plus, Inc. 60 Riverside Dr., Suite 110 New York, NY 10024	Fs, MK, S
Metropolitan Museum of Art P.O. Box 255 Gracie Station New York, NY 10028	MC, S Catalog subscription service
Milton-Bradley Educational Division 74 Park Street Springfield, MA 01101	G
The M.I.T. Press 20 Carleton Street Cambridge, MA 02142	MK, A.I.A. publications
Museum Collections Dept. S. Box 999 Radio City Station New York, NY 10019	F3d
Museum of Fine Arts 479 Huntington Avenue Boston, MA 02115	MC, S
Museum of Modern Art Publications Sales Department 11 West 53rd Street New York, NY 10019	MC, S
Museum Reproductions 3034 West Main Street Alhambra, CA 91801	Pc, F3d, inexpensive cast reproductions
National Art Education Association 1916 Association Drive Reston, VA 22091	MK, S. F2d, SSP
National Public Radio Customer Service Dept. P.O. Box 818 Niles, MI 49120	Cassettes

National Geographic Society Educational Services Department 1055 17th & M Streets NW Washington, DC 20036	Fs, MK, Ph, S
The Extension Service National Gallery of Art 6th and Constitution, NW Washington, DC 20565	Fs, MC, Pc, S
Preservation Shops National Trust for Historic Preservation 740 Jackson Place N.W. Washington, DC 20006	F2d, F3d, MC, American historical materials
New York Graphic Society 140 Greenwich Avenue Greenwich, CT 06831	F2d, Study prints
NI-WO-DI-HI Galleries Attn: J. Whitehorse P.O. Box 746 Austin, TX 78767	Fao, Native American imagery
Oestreicher's Prints, Inc. 43 West 46th Street New York, NY 10036	F2d, SSP
One of a Kind P.O. Box 1393 Aspen, CO 81612	"Impressionists" card game
Ontario Institute for Studies In Education 252 Bloor Street West Toronto, Ontario, M55 1V6, Canada	Fs, MK, Po, "10 Years In A Box" kit
Original Print Collector's Group, Ltd. 120 East 56th Street New York, NY 10022	Fao, original art work (prints)
Pace Editions, Inc. 115 E. 23rd Street New York, NY 10010	Po, Fao
Parker Brothers 50-T Dunham Road Beverly, MA 01915	G (Masterpiece, etc.)
Peabody Museum Harvard University Cambridge, MA 02128	MC

Philatelic Marketing Division U.S. Post Office, Rm. 5630 475 L'Enfant Plaza West, S.W. Washington, DC 20260	Ps
Phi Delta Kappa Eight & Union, P.O. Box 789 Bloomington, IN 47402	Fs (SWRL elementary art program)
Penn Prints 31 West 46th Street New York, NY 10036	F2d, SSP
Pflaum/Standard 8121 Hamilton Avenue Cincinnati, OH 45231	Fs, MK, Po
Philadelphia Museum of Art Benjamin Franklin Parkway at 26th St. Philadelphia, PA 19101	MC, S
The Phillips Collection 1600 East 21st Street Washington, DC 20009	MC, S
Plume Trading and Sales Co., Inc. P.O. Box 585 Monroe, NY 10950	Native American materials
Frederick A. Praeger, Inc. 111 Fourth Avenue New York, NY 10003	F2d, SSP
Price/Stern/Sloan Publications, Inc. 410 North La Cienega Boulevard Los Angeles, CA 90048	Coloring books, cultural, historical imagery
E. M. Priebat Company, Inc. P.O. Box 403 Greenwich, CT 06830	Pc (international importers of museum postcards)
Prothmann Associates, Inc. 650 Thomas Avenue Baldwin, Long Island, NY 11510	S
Remington Art Memorial Ogdensburg, NY 13669	MC
Rosenthal Art Slides 5456 S. Ridgewood Court Chicago, IL 60615	S
Sandak, Inc. 180 Harvard Avenue Stamford, CT 06902	MK, S, Thematic slide sets

Saskia Photographic Services P.O. Box K North Amherst, MS 01059	S
Scala Fine Arts Publishers, Inc. 28 West 44th Street New York, NY 10036	MK, S
Alfred Schiftan, Inc. 460 Park Avenue, South New York, NY 10016	F2d, SSP
Scholastic Magazines, Inc. 900 Sylvan Avenue Englewood Cliffs, NJ 07632	S, F2d, Folios of student work
Science Service, Inc. Things of Science 1719 N. Street NW Washington, DC 20036	MK, Individual kits
Shorewood Reproductions, Inc. 10 East 53rd Street New York, NY 10022	MK, Po, F2d, SSP
Smithsonian Institution P.O. Box 1641 Washington, DC 20013	MC, S
Photographic Services Division Smithsonian Institution Washington, DC 20560	MK, S, Thematic slide sets/ American history
Sormani Box 403 Greenwich, CT 06830	F3d, IC, Imported calendars
The St. Louis Art Museum Forest Park St. Louis, MO 63310	MC, S
Through the Flower Corporation P.O. Box 1876 Santa Monica, CA 90406	Women's art, Po, S, Pc, Fao
Time/Life Education, Inc. P.O. Box 834—Radio City Post Office New York, NY 10019	Fs, F2d, MK, S
Trident Production, Inc. 27 East 39 Street New York, NY 10016	F3d, *Netsuke* reproductions

Troubador Press 126 Folsom Street San Francisco, Ca 94105	Coloring books, Cultural, historical imagery
Uni Pub Box 433 Murray Hill Station New York, NY 10016	MK
University of Pennsylvania University Museum 33rd and Spruce Streets Philadelphia, PA 19104	MC, S
The University Prints 21 East Street Winchester, MA 10890	F2d, SSP
U.S. Committee for UNICEF 331 East 38th Street New York, NY 10016	IC, Po, International children's art
Usborne Publishing 20 Garrick Street London WC2E 9BJ, England	Time Traveller booklets and other publications
Van Nostrand Reinhold Company 450 West 33rd Street New York, NY 10001	F2d, MK, S, "Reinhold Visuals", "Look & See" series
Visual Publications, Inc. P.O. Box 297, North Main Street Champlain, NY 12919	Fs
Wadsworth Atheneum 600 Main Street Hartford, CT 06103	MC, S
Walters Art Gallery 600 North Charles Street Baltimore, MD 21201	MC, S
Warren Schloat Productions, Inc. Pleasantville, NY 10570	Fs, MK, S
Whitney Museum of American Art Madison Avenue and 75th Street New York, NY 10016	MC, S
Workshop For Learning Things, Inc. 5 Bridge Street Watertown, ME 02172	MK, Construction materials

Young Collectors Incorporated
Post Office Box 894
Haverhill, MA 01830

F3d, historical
reproductions

Check your library for EPIE publications about evaluations of the types of materials noted above or write: Educational Products Information Exchange Institute, 463 West Street, New York, NY 10014

EVALUATING INSTRUCTIONAL MATERIALS

Program leaders and designers, teachers, and others concerned with evaluating materials for classroom use need criteria to help select instructional materials. Such criteria systems are generally available in audio-visual books and periodicals, though they are often confusing because different authors suggest different criteria. Following are examples of forms that can be used to evaluate appropriateness and adequacy of instructional materials for students and teachers. All materials selected for use should be appropriate to a program's goals and needs of artistically talented students in the program, as well as adequate in terms of content and quality of materials and presentation. Figures 38 and 39 in Appendix C are based upon different methods of, and purposes for, evaluation. Figure 38 is a checklist that can be used to judge suitability of an instructional resource to a specific program and students enrolled in a program. This checklist is global and generalized and quickly guides a decision about a material's appropriateness. Figure 39 is more specific, in a number of categories, and can be used to judge an instructional material's adequacy in respect to its educational value. We used criteria on the checklist and evaluation forms (Figures 38 and 39) to help select and evaluate available instructional materials listed in this book.

CONCLUSION

The needs, abilities, and interests of artistically talented students, as they relate to atypical group and individual inquiry about the visual arts, were considered in choosing currently available educational materials. The materials listed are merely selected aids for developing small group and individual instruction for students talented in the visual arts. We do not believe that a program for artistically talented students should be designed or based upon exclusive use of commercially prepared materials. Selection of any commercially available educational material should be based upon students' needs, interests, and abilities and a program's philosophy, goals, and objectives as well as each teacher's approach to teaching. The materials listed, therefore, are intended to help artistically talented students and their teachers increase their awareness and understanding of the potentialities and richness tht study of the visual arts can bring.

APPENDIXES

IU Summer Arts Institute students are required to draw in a sketch book during the duration of the Institute. This sketch book drawing, by a ninth-grade student, is representative of the popularity of super-hero drawings done by talented adolescent students. Photo by Loret Falkner.

APPENDIX A: SAMPLE FORMS used by
the INDIANA UNIVERSITY SUMMER ARTS INSTITUTE

IU SUMMER ARTS INSTITUTE
June 16-June 28, 1985

I.U. Summer Arts Institute

Figure 1. Logo design by a college art student (left) and a participant (right).

IU SUMMER ARTS INSTITUTE ━━━━━━━━━━
School .of Education 002
Indiana University
Bloomington, IN 47405

TEACHERS, PRINCIPALS, AND COUNSELORS

A limited number of places are available for the Studio Arts and Computer

Graphics classes in the 1986 IU Summer Arts Institute. We invite you to

recommend artistically talented students in your school who meet the IU

Summer Arts Institute criteria. These should be only those students

entering grades seven through eleven this Fall and who meet at least three

of the following criteria:

- highly interested in one or more of the visual arts

- experiences in participating in one or more of the visual arts

- highly motivated and self-confident in one or more of the arts

- achievement test scores at least two grades higher than the

  student's present grade

- measured, above-average intelligence

- presently placed in a local gifted and talented school program

Each student you recommend on this form will receive an invitation to apply

to the IU Summer Arts Institute and we will indicate that you have recom-

mended the student. In order to do this, we must receive a complete home

address, including Zip code, for each student you nominate. Please list

your nominations on the back of this letter and return the nominations to

us before March 1, 1986.

Thank you,

Gilbert Clark

Gilbert Clark, Director
and the IU Summer Arts Institute Staff

Figure 2a. Teacher nomination form.

IU SUMMER ARTS INSTITUTE ━━━━━━━━━━━━

IU SUMMER ARTS INSTITUTE

NOMINATION FORM

_____   _____
Your name   _____

                                       _____
_____
Your position   School name and address

I recommend the following students who have met the criteria and show high
potential for successful participation in the IU Summer Arts Institute:

              NAME   ADDRESS, including Zip code

1. _____   _____

                                       _____

2. _____   _____

                                       _____

3. _____   _____

                                       _____

4. _____   _____

                                       _____

5. _____   _____

                                       _____

6. _____   _____

                                       _____

7. _____   _____

                                       _____

8. _____   _____

                                       _____

Figure 2b. Teacher nomination form.

IU SUMMER ARTS INSTITUTE ———————————
Education 002
Indiana University
Bloomington, IN   47405

Dear

    I want to thank you for your response to our request for student
nominations. Your support is crucial to the success of our program.
Each student you nominated has been mailed a program brochure and an
invitation to apply to the program.

    Please feel welcome to visit the Summer Arts Institute at Indiana
University, during June 22 - July 3 and to see the program in operation.
If one or more of your students are participants, you may want to see
how they work in the Summer Arts Institute situation.

    A reminder: I am offering a 3 week, 3 credit hour course, Z510
Arts for Exceptional Children: Gifted, and a 3 credit hour practicum,
Z700 for in-service teachers and graduate students, that will coincide
with the I.U. Summer Arts Institute. People who enroll will study
artistic giftedness and participate in many activities of the Summer
Arts Institute.

                  Sincerely,

                  Gilbert A. Clark
                  Director

GAC/dh

Figure 3. Teacher thank-you letter.

IU SUMMER ARTS INSTITUTE ⎯⎯⎯⎯⎯⎯⎯⎯⎯⎯⎯⎯

Education 002
3rd and Jordan
Bloomington, IN   47405
(812) 335-8549

Dear Parent;

    Your child has been nominated by the art teacher at his or her school,
to participate in the Indiana University Summer Arts Institute. We hope
that talented children, like yours, can take advantage of this exciting program for students with talents in the arts.

    Please look over the enclosed program description and discuss this with
your child. If you have questions, feel free to call the IU Department
of Art Education, (812) 335-8549. We look forward to your child's participation. If you would like to receive more information and the required application forms, please send the attached form as soon as possible.

                                        Sincerely,

                                        Gilbert Clark

                                     Gilbert Clark, Director
                                     I.U. Summer Arts Institute

----

Yes, I am interested. I would like to receive an application form for my son/
daughter to attend the IU Summer Arts Institute.

_____
Name of Child

_____
Name of Parent

_____
Home Address

_____
Parent's Signature

Mail this form to: I.U. Summer Arts Institute, Art Education Department,
School of Education 002,   Indiana University, Bloomington, IN 47405.

Figure 4. Letter to parents of nominated students.

SIXTH ANNUAL

IU SUMMER ARTS INSTITUTE ━━━━━━━━━━

SUMMER ENRICHMENT PROGRAM FOR

YOUNG PEOPLE TALENTED IN

THE ARTS

JUNE 22 - JULY 3, 1986

Sponsored by: Office of Summer Sessions; School of Education, Department of
Art Education; and the Indiana Department of Public Instruction.

Indiana University's Department of Art Education will offer a unique visual
arts program, including computer graphics, studio arts, and music, dance, and
drama classes for artistically talented students who will be entering grades
seven through eleven this Fall. For two weeks, 65 students will live in a
university dormitory or commute to the Indiana University campus and be
offered opportunities to explore and expand their talents and abilities in
the university environment. Students will attend a variety of visual arts
major classes and participate in many rewarding elective art classes and
evening programs designed for their particular interests and needs.

★★★★★★★★★★★★

A complete recreation program, including visits to museums, artists' studios,
libraries, and recreational facilities, is an important part of the program.
A residence director, recreation director, and a number of counselors will
direct afternoon, evening, and residence aspects of the program.

★★★★★★★★★★★★

Faculty members from Indiana University's Department of Art Education will be
responsible for course development, selection of enrichment activities, and
administration of the IU Summer Arts Institute. Dr. Gilbert Clark will
direct the institute. Dr. Enid Zimmerman will coordinate the institute and
the studio arts program; Dr. Guy Hubbard will coordinate the computer graphics
program. These, and other faculty members in visual arts, computer graphics,
music, dance, and drama will teach courses for the IU Summer Arts Institute.

★★★★★★★★★★★★

Figure 5a. Application packet: cover letter.

 **IU SUMMER ARTS INSTITUTE** ————————————

Participants select Computer Graphics or Studio Arts as a major area of interest. Major courses are offered from 1:30-3:30 pm daily. Elective courses are selected from several options in Visual Arts, Music, Dance, or Drama by any student. Electives, scheduled from 8:00-10:00 am and 11:00 am-12:00 daily, enable students to attend two different electives classes. From 3:30-5:30 pm, participants are offered an organized recreation program, with instructors, to include swimming and other outdoor sports. In the evening, there will be a series of arts programs featuring professional artists and performers. Some weekend and evening activities include concerts, museum visits, and opportunities to become familiar with the arts facilities on the IU campus such as the IU Library, Musical Arts Center, IU Art Museum, and The Lilly Library. There is also time for leisure activities, making new friends, and just relaxing.

VISUAL ARTS MAJOR CLASSES WILL INCLUDE:
COMPUTER GRAPHICS (limited to 20 students)

APPLE ART Generating computer graphics on microcomputers

STUDIO ARTS (limited to 45 students)

Drawing and Painting I Developing drawing and painting skills and generating and elaborating ideas.
Drawing and Painting II Developing advanced drawing and painting skills and generating individual techniques.

VISUAL ARTS ELECTIVES

Photography Exploring the many possibilities of camera and cameraless photography.
Ink and Paper Developing printmaking skills.
3D Forms Developing skills in making sculpture with a variety of 3D media, including clay.
Epics & Sagas Drawing as a means of story telling.
Figure Drawing Learning to draw portraits and the human figure.

Figure 5a. Cover letter, continued.

IU SUMMER ARTS INSTITUTE ═══════════════════

MUSIC ELECTIVES

> Choral Music Exploring group singing techniques.
>
> Musical Theater Putting together a musical show.

DANCE ELECTIVES

> Jazz Dance Relating jazz music and dance techniques.
>
> Dance Improvisation Developing spontaneity and creative movement
> in dance performance.

DRAMA ELECTIVES

> Drama Workshop Developing skills of characterization and presentation
> for the theater.
>
> Mime Improvisation Using pantomime techniques for creating drama.

I.U. Resident Life:

- All participants will be supervised by trained, adult counselors. One
  counselor will be responsible for every twelve students.
- Participants will either live in a University Residence Hall where two
  participants will share a room or commute to the Indiana University campus.
- Meals will be served in a Residence Hall cafeteria that offers several
  choices each meal. Non-resident participants will receive lunch and
  participate in all classes and have the option of attending evening activities.
- A Director-in-Residence and counselors will live in the Residence Hall with
  resident-participants.
- A Registered Nurse will be on 24 hour call and emergency care will be
  provided by the Bloomington Hospital.
- A central office for the I U Summer Arts Institute will be maintained on
  a 24 hour basis throughout the duration of the program.
- Pay telephones will be provided for out-going long distance calls by
  participants.

Figure 5a. Cover letter, continued.

IU SUMMER ARTS INSTITUTE ────────

TUITION

A $450.00 fee, per student, will cover costs of instruction, materials,
recreation, housing and meals, medical care, counselors and counseling, and
access to various University resources. A $275.00 fee, per student, is
offered for non-residential students who commute to Indiana University.
Non-residential participants will receive lunch and attend all classes and
related activities. The fee for out-of-state students is $475.00.

APPLICATION DEADLINE IS APRIL 18, 1986

In order to apply for this program, a $50.00 deposit must accompany this
application. The balance must be remitted by June 1, 1986 if the student
is accepted. Please make a check or money order payable to:

Indiana University Conference #298-86.

Requests for refunds must be made in writing to the Conference Bureau. No
refunds will be made after June 9, 1986.

A limit of 65 participants will be selected for the IU Summer Arts Institute.
They will be notified of acceptance by May 2, 1986. Those not selected will
be notified and their deposits returned on the same date.

For further information, including schedules of courses, enrichment opportunities, and recreational activities, contact the Department of Art Education,
School of Education 002, Bloomington, IN 47405; (812) 335-8549.

The YELLOW form is to be completed by the parent or guardian.

The BLUE form is to be completed by the student.

The GREEN form is to be completed by the school principal, counselor, and
art specialist or other teacher.

All forms are to be returned, together with a $50.00 deposit to:
IU Summer Arts Institute, School of Education 002, Indiana University,
Bloomington, IN 47405. (812) 335-8549

Figure 5a. Cover letter, continued.

STUDENT'S INFORMATION FORM (BLUE FORM)

IU SUMMER ARTS INSTITUTE ───────────────
Education 002
Indiana University
Bloomington, IN 47405

To be completed by the applicant:

Your name_____

Sex_____ Birthdate_____
                            (month)   (day)   (year)

Home address_____

City_____State_____Zip Code_____Phone_____

Check grade you will be entering in the fall:

7th____ 8th____ 9th____ 10th____ 11th____

Check one of the following major areas of interest:

_____Studio Arts I   _____Studio Arts II   _____Apple Art
Drawing/Painting   Advanced Drawing &   Computer Graphics
                          Painting

Rank, in order of preference (1-4), four of the following elective courses.
Participants will be enrolled in two elective courses and will be awarded
their preferences as nearly as possible.

_____Figure Drawing   _____Musical Theatre

_____Photography   _____Jazz Dance

_____Ink and Paper   _____Dance Improvisation

_____3-D Forms   _____Drama Workshop

_____Epics & Sagas   _____Mime Improvisation

_____Choral Music

On the back of this form, please describe, briefly, your special interests
and previous activities in the arts.

Figure 5b. Student's information form (blue).

PARENTS INFORMATION (YELLOW FORM)

IU SUMMER ARTS INSTITUTE _____

Education 002
Indiana University
Bloomington, IN 47405

Student's Name_____

Sex_____ Birthdate_____

                                 (month)   (day)   (year)

Home Address_____

City_____State_____Zip Code___ ___ Phone_____

Name of School_____

School System_____

Teacher's Name_____Principal's Name_____

Father's or Guardian's Name_____

Occupation_____Business Phone_____

Mother's or Guardian's Name_____

Occupation_____Business Phone_____

Alternate contact person
(in case of emergency) ─────────────────────── Phone_____

Is student currently enrolled in a program for gifted & talented? Yes____No____

If yes, name of program_____

Type of program_____hours/week_____

Has applicant attended a previous Visual & Performing Arts Summer Program?

Yes_____ No_____ ; Name of program_____

Briefly describe previous arts experiences of the applicant:

_____

_____

_____

_____

How did you learn about the Summer Arts Institute?_____

_____

_____

Figure 5c. Parent's information form (yellow).

NOMINATION FCRM (GREEN FORM)

IU SUMMER ARTS INSTITUTE ━━━━━━━━━━━━
Education 002
Indiana University
Bloomington, Indiana 47405

Criteria For Nomination

Any student entering grades seven through eleven in the Fall, and who meets
at least three of the following criteria may be nominated:

o highly interested in one or several of the visual arts
o experiences in participating in one of several of the visual arts
o highly motivated and self-confident in one or several of the arts
o achievement test scores at least two grades higher than the student's
  present grade
o measured, above-average intelligence
o presently placed in a local gifted and talented school program

To be completed by the applicant's principal, counselor, and art specialist
or other teacher.

Student's Name_____

Name of School_____

School Address_____

City_____State_____Zip Code_____Phone_____

Principal's Name_____

Please describe the student's major strengths and interests:_____
_____
_____
_____

Counselor or Specialist's Name_____

Please describe the student's major strengths and interests:_____
_____
_____

Teacher's Name_____ School Address_____

Please describe the student's major strengths and interests:_____
_____
_____

Please return this form to the student's parents or guardians.

Figure 5d. Nomination form (green).

IU SUMMER ARTS INSTITUTE _____
Education 002
Indiana University
Bloomington, IN 47405
(812) 335-8549

May 2, 1986

We are very pleased to invite your child to participate in this year's
IU Summer Arts Institute. The vast range of skills and abilities in this
year's group will, surely, contribute to an exciting and stimulating
experience for your child.

The programs in Studio Arts and Computer Graphics welcome young people
who have selected these majors. Electives, open to all participants, will
expand and enrich your child's summer experiences at IU. Our evening
programs and recreation activities are specifically designed for participants who will be in this program.

The balance of payment for each participant is due June 2, 1986.
Please make check or money order payable to:

> Indiana University Conference #298-86
>
> IU Conference Bureau IMU-L9
>
> Bloomington, IN 47405

Requests for refunds must be made in writing to the IU Conference Bureau.
No refunds will be made after June 9, 1986.

We look forward to your child's participation in this year's IU Summer
Arts Institute. All of the staff will do everything we can to make this an
enjoyable and rewarding experience for your child. Further information about
the IU Summer Arts Institute program is enclosed.

Sincerely,

Gilbert Clark

Gilbert Clark, Director
IU Summer Arts Institute,

Enid Zimmerman

Enid Zimmerman, Coordinator
IU Summer Arts Institute

Figure 6a. Acceptance letter to parents.

IU SUMMER ARTS INSTITUTE ═══════════════

Education 002
Indiana University
Bloomington, IN 47405

(812) 335-8549

May 2, 1986

Congratulations, you have been selected as a participant in the I U
Summer Arts Institute. We are proud of the skills and interests of the participants for this year's program. You will meet many other talented young people
when you attend the program. We believe you'll make many new friends and
enjoy the many arts activities that will be offered at the I U Summer Arts
Institute.

We look forward to your participation and contributions to the exciting
program that awaits you at Indiana University.

Sincerely,

Gilbert Clark, Director
I U Summer Arts Institute
Enid Zimmerman, Coordinator
I U Summer Arts Institute

Figure 6b. Acceptance letter to applicants.

 **IU SUMMER ARTS INSTITUTE** ⎯⎯⎯⎯⎯⎯⎯⎯

Dear

    We appreciate your child's application to the IU Summer Arts Institute.
Unfortunately, we are not able to offer a place in the 1986 program.
There was an overwhelming response to this year's Institute; due to the
number of applicants and limited number of spaces in the program, we were
not able to place your child.

    We encourage you to have your child apply to next year's IU Summer Arts
Institute before the deadline and to continue to support his or her interest
in the arts. We appreciate your past support and interest in the IU Summer
Art Institute and hope we can include your child in next year's Institute.

                                        Sincerely,

                                        Gilbert Clark
                                        Gilbert Clark, Director

                                        Enid Zimmerman
                                        Enid Zimmerman, Coordinator

Figure 7. Rejection letter.

In order to enable the Student Health Service of Indiana University at Bloomington to provide prompt care to your minor son or daughter, we urge you to read and complete this consent form, and see to its prompt return to the program sponsor so that, in case of need, we can help your child without delay.

CONSENT FOR MEDICAL TREATMENT OF A MINOR

I, _____ , declare that I am the
          (Full name of parent/guardian)

_____ , of _____ ,
          (Father/Mother/Guardian)   (Full name of minor)
a minor, age _____ , born _____ , 19_____ . I grant permission to the

Director Assistants, or other persons responsible for his/her care to act on my behalf

for said minor in granting permission for evaluation and treatment of medical problems.

I UNDERSTAND THAT SHOULD A MAJOR MEDICAL PROBLEM ARISE, AN ATTEMPT WILL BE MADE TO NOTIFY ME BY TELEPHONE. IN THE EVENT THAT I CANNOT BE REACHED, I HEREBY GIVE MY CONSENT TO SUCH MEDICAL TREATMENT AS DEEMED NECESSARY, INCLUDING SURGERY, X-RAY EXAMINATIONS AND ANESTHESIA TO BE RENDERED TO SAID MINOR BY A LICENSED PHYSICIAN OR NURSE.

I hereby certify that I have read and fully understand this authorization.

Date:_____ Signature:_____
                                                      (Parent or Guardian)

IN CASE OF EMERGENCY: Telephone: (Home) _____/_____

                                            (Work) _____/_____

                             Address: _____

                                            _____

Please provide the following additional information concerning said minor:

   Allergic Reactions: _____

   Present Medication (if taking now): _____

   Date of last Tetanus Toxoid: _____

   Any past illnesses or other information that would be useful in the event medical
   treatment is necessary:_____

I do not wish medical care of any kind except emergency care to be provided for:	I authorize limited medical care to be provided for: _____
	As follows:_____
_____	_____
Signature of Parent or Guardian	_____
	Signature of Parent or Guardian
Date:_____	Date:_____

Figure 8. Consent for medical treatment form.

IU SUMMER ARTS INSTITUTE ━━━━━━━━━━━━━━━

To all Residential Participants:

As guests of Indiana University, you will be subject to conduct standards
of IU. Most of the rules simply call for respect of other students and
their needs. We share our dormitory with other institutes that use the
dorm for small classes and study hours as well as a residence. The
dormitory is home for a lot of people who need to study.

All IUSAI participants will remain on campus and be supervised by Institute
staff members at all times.

Participants will observe quiet hours (9:30 pm - 7:30 am) and floor
assignments. After evening activities, there will be NO open visiting
in the residence hall. Boys are not permitted on girl's floor and girls
are not permitted on boys floors.

After 10:00 pm we must insist on quiet in the hallways and rooms. NO loud
radios or talking will be permitted after 10:00 pm.

Participants will not use the residence hall stairs or stairwell. The
stairs are for emergency use only. All floor changes will be by elevator.

NO food or drink will be ordered or delivered into the residence hall
without the express permission of the Head Counselor.

I have read the rules of IUSAI residence and I agree to abide by these rules.

_____   _____
Date   Student's signature

I have read the rules of IUSAI residence and I agree that my son/daughter
should abide by these rules

_____   _____
Date   Parent/Guardian signature

Figure 9. Rules of conduct form.

Clothing Inventory

Student's Name _____

I. Beginning Inventory   II. Ending Inventory

    by _____   by _____

    Date _____   Date _____

<u>Description</u>
(color, size, etc.)

Number   Number

_____ Blouses   _____

_____ Shirts   _____

_____ Pants   _____

_____ Slacks   _____

_____ Shorts   _____

_____ Shoes/Tennis shoes   _____

_____ Socks   _____

_____ Underwear   _____

_____ Pajamas   _____

_____ Jacket/Sweater/Sweatshirt   _____

_____ Raincoat/Hat   _____

_____ Bathing suit/Cap   _____

_____ Toothbrush/Paste   _____

_____ Deodorant/Shampoo/Soap   _____

_____ Comb/Brush   _____

_____ Bath towel   _____

_____ Soap powders (Laundry)   _____

_____ Suitcase   _____

_____ Sports Equipment (OPTIONAL)   _____

_____ Instruments (OPTIONAL)   _____

_____ Board Games/Hobbies   _____

_____ Notebooks, Pens, Pencils, Stamps, Envelopes, etc.   _____

_____ Other   _____

_____ Other   _____

Figure 10. Clothing inventory.

IU SUMMER ARTS INSTITUTE ──────────────

Dear Parents,

We will be taking group and individual photographs for professional presentations and for publicity purposes. Selected photographs and slides will be shown on Friday, July 3 at our closing activities. We need your consent for public showing of these images.

A Proffitt Foundation research grant has been awarded to Dr. Guskin and Dr. Zimmerman to study the effects of "labeling" students as gifted or talented. These faculty need your permission to administer a questionnaire to each IUSAI participant. All reporting will be generalized; individual student's names will never be used in the reporting of this research.

Please sign the following consent form:

I hereby give permission for my child, _____,

to be photographed in IUSAI activities and to be administered a research

questionnaire during the IUSAI.

```
                                    _____
                                    Signature              Date
```

Figure 11. Research photograph release form.

 **IU SUMMER ARTS INSTITUTE** ══════════════

1986 Program Contract

TO:_____

ADDRESS (campus)_____

OTHER ADDRESS_____

TELEPHONE_____

SOCIAL SECURITY #_____

This is confirmation of your agreement to serve as_____

for the 1986 IU Summer Arts Institute. The dates of this year's Institute are

June 22 through July 3, 1986. You will be required to attend two short

planning meetings prior to the program dates.

Payment for services will be $_____ for the two week period.

                                           _____

                                           Gilbert A. Clark, Director   Date

****

I agree to the conditions set forth in this contract with the 1986 IU Summer

Arts Institute.

                                           _____

                                           Staff Member   Date

Figure 12. Program contract.

IU SUMMER ARTS INSTITUTE ━━━━━━━━━━━━━━

JOB DESCRIPTION FOR PROGRAM TEACHER

Function:

Under supervision of the Director and Coordinator, each teacher is responsible for the planning and carrying out of a two week instructional program, including ordering and supervision of supplies, responsibility for students during all instructional periods, and evaluation of instructional program.

Example of Duties:

- Organize an instructional program that will excite students and challenge their skills and abilities to express artistic statements.

- Act as an instructional advisor to IUSAI students in their classes to promote learning and growth of skills and abilities.

- Be responsible for class groups during instructional periods, including breaks and after instruction, until groups are taken over by another staff member.

- Keep accurate records of class activities as a part of evaluation records.

- Be responsible for classroom management of supplies and materials and for classroom clean-up following class.

- Make and communicate rules and regulations for safety and respect of other classes that are concurrently in session.

- Secure needed supplies, materials, and equipment (including AV equipment) prior to instructional classes.

- Attend a workshop before the Institute begins and meet with the director and coordinator during the Institute.

Figure 13a. Job description for program teacher.

IU SUMMER ARTS INSTITUTE ━━━━━━━━━━

JOB DESCRIPTION FOR PROGRAM COUNSELOR

Function:

Under supervision of a Head-Counselor, each counselor is responsible for a group of participants, one or more activities of a residential program, and related work as required:

Examples of Duties:

- Organize, promote, and lead one or more early evening recreational activities such as games, poetry, or studio activities.

- Be in charge of a group of participants in the residential center and act as an advisor, counselor, and manager of a group of participants.

- Assist in the delivery of students to the instructional program (8:00 am), pick-up of students from mid-day instructional classes for lunch and bring them to afternoon instructional classes, and pick up students at end of instructional classes (3:30 pm).

- Promote, organize and stimulate good relationships among counselors, staff, participants, and other people on the IU campus.

- Make and communicate rules and regulations for safety and welfare of participants in cooperation with the Head Counselor.

- Secure needed equipment and supplies necessary to conduct recreation activities.

- Reside and eat in residential center with participants.

- Report to Head Counselor on schedule of activities, participants, plans, programs, problems, and needs. Recommend actions and carry out policies and objectives of the afternoon and evening program.

- Coordinate and assist in conduct of special evening events.

- Assist in the evaluation of program and make recommendations for next year's program.

- Attend a workshop before the Institute begins and meet with the director and coordinator during the Institute.

Figure 13b. Job description for program counselor.

IU SUMMER ARTS INSTITUTE ━━━━━━━━━━━

STUDENT EVALUATION FORM

NAME_____

1. Which classes did you take? Circle the names:

   Ink & Paper   Drama Workshop   Epics & Sagas
   Clay   Dance Improv   Photography
   Drawing & Painting I Drawing & Painting II   Apple Art

2. Which classes did you like best?_____

   Why?_____

   _____

   _____

3. What Evening Programs did you like best? Circle the names:

   A. Rainbow   B. Tibetan Pilgrimage   C. Circle Walker

   D. Sat. Nite Dance E. Talent Show   F. Photo Talk

   G. Jeff Foster   H. Movies

   Why?_____

   _____

   _____

4. What recreation activities did you like best?   Why?_____

   _____

   _____

   _____

5. If you could change some things about the Summer Arts Institute for next
   summer, what changes would you make?_____

   _____

   _____

PLEASE PUT ADDITIONAL COMMENTS ON BACK OF PAPER

Figure 14a. Student evaluation form.

IU SUMMER ARTS INSTITUTE _____

FACULTY EVALUATION FORM

Name_____Class_____

1. What activities do you think were most successful in the class you
   taught? Why were they successful?_____

   _____

   _____

   _____

2. What things would you change if you were to teach this same class next
   summer?_____

   _____

   _____

   _____

Additional Comments:

Figure 14b. Faculty evaluation form.

IU SUMMER ARTS INSTITUTE ━━━━━━━━━━━━━

COUNSELOR'S EVALUATION FORM

Name_____

1. What were the most successful aspects of the Institute?_____

    _____

    _____

    Why?_____

    _____

    _____

2. What recommendations do you suggest for next year's program? Consider all
    areas of the Institute's activities such as suggestions for the educational
    classes, recreation program, dormitory life for the participants, transporting
    of participants, communications, and load requirements for participants and
    counselors.

    _____

    _____

    _____

    _____

    _____

    _____

Figure 14c. Counselor evaluation form.

IU SUMMER ARTS INSTITUTE ════════════

I.U. Summer Arts Institute
Parent Evaluation

1. What were your child's overall impressions of the two week experience? What kinds of words were used to describe the program?

2. What experience was talked about the most? Why was this experience remembered most vividly?

3. In the I U Summer Arts Institute, the children studied several classes with several different teachers.

   3a. What classes were remembered most positively? What reasons were given for this reaction?

   3b. What teachers were remembered most positively? What reasons were given for this reaction?

4. As a parent or guardian, your reactions and suggestions for future programs are important to our planning. On the bottom of this sheet, please describe your reactions to the program (based upon what you observed and upon conversations with your child) and please give us your suggestions for offering a better program in the future. What should be the same? What should be changed? What should we offer that was not offered this year? How can we improve the program, for other children, in the future? If we offered this opportunity, would your child like to return?

Figure 14d. Parent evaluation form.

APPENDIX B: SAMPLE TESTING INSTRUMENTS
and STUDENT TEST RESPONSES

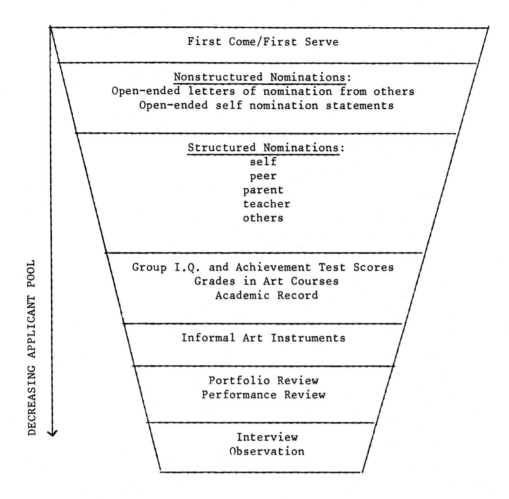

Figure 15. Screening procedures for identifying artistically talented students.

SELF—NOMINATION FORM: Visual Arts

Name _____ Grade _____

School _____ Teacher _____

                                         Age   _____

PLEASE CHECK THE STATEMENTS THAT BEST DESCRIBE YOU:

1. My classmates consider me an artist.   _____

2. My art work is among the best in my class.   _____

3. I often do artwork outside of school.   _____

4. I doodle and scribble all the time.   _____

5. I use art work to help explain my ideas.   _____

6. I like to go to art museums.   _____

7. I like to show my art work to others.   _____

8. I enjoy television programs about art and artists.   _____

9. I have done art work for my school plays, newspaper, etc. _____

10. I like to copy, or draw, cartoons.   _____

                                  _____
                                  Student signature   Date

Adapted from forms used by the Jersey City Public Schools, Rhode Island
Department of Education, and Baltimore County Public Schools.

Figure 16. Structured self-nomination checklist.

SELF-ASSESSMENT/NOMINATION FORM

Name _____   School _____

Age _____   Grade _____   Teacher _____

1. What art classes you have taken in school?

   _____

   _____

   _____

2. What art classes you have taken outside of school?

   _____

   _____

   _____

3. Describe the best art project you have ever made:

   _____

   _____

   _____

4. What other activities do you enjoy, besides art activities?

   _____

   _____

   _____

5. What are our special interests and talents in art?

   _____

   _____

   _____

Figure 17. Structured self-assessment/nomination form.

6. I am interested in participating in the Visual Arts Program because:

_____

_____

_____

_____

_____

_____

Adapted from forms used by the Chesterfield (VA) County Public Schools,
Arkansas Governor's School, Connecticut State Department of Education, School
Board of Pinellas County (FL).

Figure 17. Structured self-assessment/nomination form, continued.

PEER NOMINATION FORM: Visual Arts

Name _____   School _____

Age _____   Grade _____   Teacher _____

Write the names of your classmates that best fit the following questions:

1. Who spends the most time drawing in and out of the art class?

_____   _____

2. Who would you ask to design a poster for the school play?

_____   _____

3. If you were assigned a group art project, who would you most like to work with?

_____   _____

4. Who thinks of the most unusual, fantastic, or original ideas?

_____   _____

5. Who spends the most time working on their art projects?

_____   _____

6. Who sets the highest standards for his or her art work?

_____   _____

Adapted from forms used by the Jersey City Public Schools.

Figure 18. Structured peer nomination form.

PEER NOMINATION CHECKLIST: VISUAL ARTS

Your name _____   School _____

Grade _____ Age _____   Art Teacher _____

Name of student nominated _____

School _____   Grade _____

Read the following statements carefully.   Put an X in the column that best
describes the student you have nominated.

	Seldom	Occasion-ally	Fre-quently	Almost always
1. Draws a lot in school	_____	_____	_____	_____
2. Does outstanding art work	_____	_____	_____	_____
3. Uses many different materials to do art work	_____	_____	_____	_____
4. Makes art outside of school	_____	_____	_____	_____
5. Enjoys talking about art	_____	_____	_____	_____
6. Has many original ideas about art	_____	_____	_____	_____

Additional comments about your nominee:

_____

_____

_____

Adapted from forms used by the Baltimore (MD) County Public Schools.

Figure 19. Structured peer nomination checklist.

PARENT NOMINATION AND RATING FORM

Name of Nominee _____

Address _____

Age _____   Grade _____   Teacher _____

The Visual Arts Program needs you help in identifying students with special abilities in the arts. Please check ( ) the column that best describes your child. All information you provide will be held in strictest confidence.

	Seldom	Occasion-ally	Fre-quently	Almost always
1. Creates art work at home				
2. Wants to visit exhibitions, art museums, or crafts shows				
3. Likes to share his/her art work				
4. Is asked by others to do art work				
5. Is interested in how things look in the home and community				
6. Uses spending money to buy art supplies or books				
7. Admires the art work of others				
8. Seeks help to improve his/her art work				

Additional comments:

_____

_____

_____

_____

_____   _____
Signature of parent   Date

Adapted from forms used in the Baltimore (MD) County Public Schools.

Figure 20. Structured parent nomination form.

Art Behavior Checklist

Nomination Form

	Seldom	Occasionally	Frequently	Always
Name of Student				
School Grade				
1. Is more apt to respond to artistic peer and adult role models				
2. Possesses a well developed visual memory				
3. Possesses a high curiosity level that stimulates active imagination				
4. Is more apt to respond to environmental observations and changes				
5. Is capable of original thinking				
6. Has the ability to generalize				
7. Examines problems critically				
8. Is able to concentrate for long periods of time				
9. Seeks challenging experiences that are goal – oriented				
10. Engages in compulsive pursuit of special interests				
11. Imposes self-criticism that interferes with satisfaction with task				
Column Total	___	___	___	___
Weight	1	2	3	4
Weighted Column Total	___	___	___	___

Nominator _____

Title _____   OVERALL TOTAL   _____

Date _____

Additional comments: _____

_____

_____

Adapted from "Charactistics List", Project Art Band: A Program For Visually Gifted Children. Lincoln, M.A.: DeCordova Museum, 1982.

Figure 21. Structured art behavior checklist.

VISUAL ARTS ASSESSMENT FORM

Student's Name _____ Grade _____

School _____ Teacher _____

Person completing form: Classroom teacher   Art teacher

                             Art specialist   Principal

                             Other _____

Circle the number in front of each statement that best describes the student you are nominating:

WORK HABITS AND LEARNING ABILITIES:

1. Shows insight; is observant

2. Masters basic art skills easily and quickly

3. Has a sense of humor; enjoys contradictions and paradoxes

4. Takes pride in own art work

5. Works independently

6. Concentrates on art projects for long periods of time.

7. Finishes art projects.

ART KNOWLEDGE AND SKILLS

8. Is critical of own art work and art work of others

9. Creates skillful, well organized compositional arrangements

10. Uses different media effectively and confidently

11. Demonstrates elaboration and depiction of details in art work

12. Creates charts, graphs, models, or other visuals to supplement work

13. Shows interest and knowledge about works of art from the past and present

DESIRE AND INTEREST

14. Spends a great deal of time, in and out of school, doing art work

15. Shows high desire for visually stimulating experiences

16. Is self-motivated, self-stimulated to make art work

Figure 22. Structured visual arts assessment form.

17. Demonstrates high desire to improve own art work

18. Shows exceptional art skills in _____

    List honors and awards nominee has received:

    _____

    _____

19. List of characteristics applicable to the nominee:

    _____

    _____

20. Why do you think this student should be recommended for the Visual Arts
    Program? _____

    _____

    _____

Adapted from forms used by Chesterfield (VA) County Public Schools and
Tonawanda (NY) Union Free School District.

Figure 22. Structured visual arts assessment form, continued.

```
Project Art Band          Student _____
De Cordova Museum         Grade _____
Lincoln, Massachusetts    School _____
                          Town _____
```

NARRATIVE DRAWING SCORING GUIDE

Objects

_____   Number of Objects
_____   Resolution of Detail in Objects (1 to 10)
_____   Proportional Accuracy within Objects (1 to 10)
_____   Relationship Appropriateness of Objects (1 to 10)
_____   Figure Animation (1 to 10)

Composition

_____   Background Resolution (1 to 10)
            Perspective
_____   Diminishing Objects (4)
_____   Overlapping Planes (6)
_____   Vanishing Points (8)
_____   Aerial (10)
_____   Textural Differentiation (1 to 10)
_____   Value - Shading (1 to 10)
_____   Use of Emphasis (1 to 10)
_____   Use of Exaggeration (1 to 10)

Story

_____   Narrative of Common Event (1)
_____   Narrative of Fantasy (2)
_____   Change of State (3)
_____   Resolution (completeness) (1 to 10)

_____   TOTAL

Figure 23. Assessment instrument developed by David W. Baker.

Figure 24a. Below average.

Figure 24b. Average.

Figure 24c. Above average.

Figure 24. Responses to Baker's Visual Narrative Assessment Instrument.

Figure 25. Scoring guide for Baker's Visual Memory Assessment Instrument.

```
Project Art Band          Student _____
De Cordova Museum         Grade _____
Lincoln, Massachusetts    School _____
                          Town _____
```

VISUAL MEMORY SCORING GUIDE _____

_____   Number of Objects Shown

_____   Perspective Shown in Floor (3)

_____   Perspective Shown in Furniture (3)

_____   Perspective Effects Shown With Accuracy (5)

_____   Attempts at Texturing Evident (3)

_____   Lines in Chair Seat Caining Shown (3)

_____   Six Wall Hangings Shown (3)

_____   Wall Hangings in Correct Positions (2)

_____   Details Shown in Wall Hangings (3)

_____   Details Shown in Wall Hangings Accurate (5)

_____   Curve of Bed Boards Shown (2)

_____   Details in Bed Board Shown (3)

_____   Details in Door Shown (2)

_____   Window Shown as Open (2)

_____   Window Grids Shown (2)

_____   Corners of Room Shown (3)

_____   Accuracy of Total Composition (1 to 10)

_____   TOTAL

Assessment Instrument Developed by David W. Baker

Figure 26. Scoring guide for Baker's Visual Memory Assessment Instrument.

Figure 27a. Below average.

Figure 27b. Average.

Figure 27c. Above average.

Figure 27. Responses to Baker's Visual Memory Assessment Instrument.

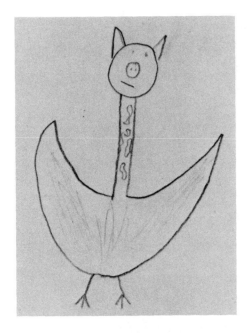

Figure 28a. Below average.

Figure 28b. Average.

Figure 28c. Above average.

Figure 28. Bellessis: Fantasy drawings.

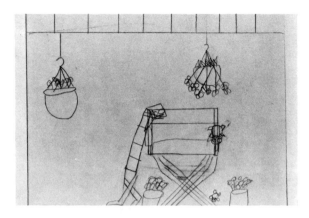

Figure 29a. Below average.

Figure 29b. Average.

Figure 29c. Above average.

Figure 29. Bellessis: Observational drawings.

Figure 30a. Below average.

Figure 30b. Average.

Figure 30c. Above average.

Figure 30. Bellessis: Dictated drawings of an aardvark.

CLARK-GARERI DRAWING INSTRUMENT

<u>Item Criteria</u>

I. SENSORY PROPERTIES

A. LINE: Nonvariation/Variation. A line may exhibit many qualities such as measure, type, direction, location, etc., regarding variation among these qualities:

1. Shows <u>no</u> variation, lines are all similar

2. <u>Most</u> lines are similar

3. <u>Half</u> of lines are varied, half are similar

4. <u>Most</u> lines are varied

5. High amount of line variation, effectively used

B. SHAPE: Nonvariation/Variation. A shape may exhibit many qualities such as outline/non-outline, size, type, location, etc., regarding variation among these qualities:

1. Shows <u>no</u> variation in shapes

2. <u>Most</u> shapes are similar, minimal variation

3. Half of shapes are varied, half are similar

4. Shapes are mostly varied

5. High amount of shape variation, effectively used

C. TEXTURE: Amount and Variety. Texture may be used to increase interest, define area, represent actual texture, etc., regarding texture among these uses:

1. Completely <u>lacking</u> or inappropriate use of texture

2. <u>Small</u> amount and variety of texture

3. Moderate amount and variety of texture

4. Good amount and variety of texture

5. All surfaces textured appropriately

Figure 31. Clark-Gareri Drawing Instrument.

D. VALUE: lightness and darkness. Value may be used to indicate a light source, shapes of objects, increase interest, add depth, etc., regarding value among these uses:

1. Shows <u>no</u> gradation of shaping or value or used inappropriately

2. <u>Small</u> amount of shading or value

3. Moderate amount of shading or value

4. Good amount of shading or value

5. High amount and appropriate use of shading or value

II. FORMAL PROPERTIES

A. RHYTHM: Repetition and Variation. Rhythm is attained by ordered or regular recurrence of sensory properties. It depicts a continuance, a flow, or a feeling of movement. In regards to rhythm:

1. Exhibits no, or inappropriate, repetition or variation

2. Exhibits small amount of rhythm

3. Exhibits moderate amount of rhythm

4. Exhibits a good amount of rhythm

5. Exhibits a high amount and appropriate use of rhythm

B. BALANCE (Appropriate amount). Balance is attained by equality of weight, attention, or attraction among the sensory properties used. In regards to balance:

1. Exhibits no sense of balance

2. Exhibits only a small amount of balance

3. Exhibits a moderate amount of balance

4. Exhibits a good amount of balance

5. Exhibits appropriate and varied balance

C. UNITY: Harmony and Variety. Unity is attained by effective harmony and variety between the sensory and other formal properties.

1. Exhibits no sense of harmony and variety

2. Exhibits a small amount of unity

Figure 31. Clark-Gareri Drawing Instrument, continued.

C. UNITY (cont'd)

    3. Exhibits a moderate amount of unity

    4. Exhibits a good amount of unity

    5. Exhibits appropriate and effective unity

D. COMPOSITION (Effectiveness). A composition is effected by any and all of its parts. In regards to composition:

    1. Ineffective composition

    2. Exhibits some sense of composition

    3. Exhibits good composition in only part of the image

    4. Exhibits good, but incomplete, composition

    5. Superior and effective overall composition

III. EXPRESSIVE PROPERTIES

A. MOOD: Dynamic states. Mood is communicated by the combined · effect of subject matter and expressive content. In regards to mood:

    1. Exhibits no evidence of mood or expression

    2. Exhibits inappropriate or incomplete evidence of mood or expression

    3. Exhibits some mood or expression in only part of the image

    4. Exhibits good but incomplete mood or expression

    5. Exhibits appropriate, effective, complete mood or expression

B. ORIGINALITY (Non-imitativeness). Originality is shown as inventiveness, unigueness, or freshness of aspect, etc., in regards to originality:

    1. Complete lack of originality, sterotyped or imitative

    2. Mainly imitative with originality in small part or parts

    3. Half original, half imitative parts

    4. Mainly original with imitative parts

    5. High degree of originality throughout

Figure 31. Clark-Gareri Drawing Instrument, continued.

IV. TECHNICAL PROPERTIES

A. TECHNIQUE/CRAFT. Technique is determined by the manners and
    skills an artist uses with tools and materials. In regard to
    technique:

    1. No evidence of technique or inappropriate use of materials

    2. Exhibits small amount of technique

    3. Exhibits moderate amount of technique

    4. Exhibits considerable amount of technique

    5. Skillful and appropriate use of technique

B. CORRECTNESS/SOLUTION TO THE PROBLEM. The Clark-Gareri Drawing
    Instrument assigns specific drawing tasks; testees can be graded
    as to the correctness to the solution of the problem:

    1. Inappropriate to the problem assigned

    2. Appropriate to the problem, but incorrectly drawn

    3. Appropriate and partially correct re: proportion, perspective,
        shading, etc.

    4. Correct to the problem assigned and drawn correctly

    5. Unusual solution, but correct to the problem assigned and
        drawn correctly

Figure 31. Clark-Gareri Drawing Instrument, continued.

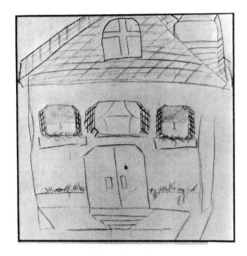

Figure 32a. Below average.

Figure 32b. Average.

Figure 32c. Above average.

Figure 32. Clark-Gareri Drawing Test: House, eighth grade.

Figure 33a. Below average.

Figure 33b. Average.

Figure 33c. Above average.

Figure 33. Clark-Gareri Drawing Test: Running person, ninth grade.

Figure 34a. Below average.

Figure 34b. Average.

Figure 34c. Above average.

Figure 34. Clark-Gareri Drawing Test: Playground, tenth grade.

ART PORTFOLIO AND PERFORMANCE REVIEW

GUIDELINES

1. Candidates must submit a portfolio that includes 6-8 pieces of
   art work. Color slides may be used only for 3-D, sculptural
   works. No works copied from photographs or the works of other
   artists or designers may be included; the contents are expected
   to be original and creative works by the candidate. Art works
   represent three or more of the following:
   A. Pencil, charcoal, conté crayon, or chalk, 12"x18" minimum.
   B. Ink and pen, 9"x12" minimum.
   C. Watercolor, 12"x18" minimum.
   D. Figure studies in any medium, 12"x18" minimum.
   E. 3-D, sculptural work any size, colorslides may be submitted.
   F. Choice of subject and medium, 12"x18" minimum.

2. All portfolios will be evaluated with the following criteria:
   A. Creativity and originality, expressiveness of content.
   B. Skillful use of elements and principles of design.
   C. Appropriate techniques with tools and materials.
   D. Overall quality of the art works.
   E. Evidence of concentration and personal committment.

3. Portfolios will be screened by judges; selected applicants will be
   invited to return to complete the following procedures:
   A. Selected applicants will be asked to take a short drawing test
      supervised by judges.
   B. Selected applicants will be asked to complete two art assignments
      while observed by judges.
   C. Selected applicants will be asked to discuss the art works in
      their portfolios with judges.

All candidates are expected to have different backgrounds in art and
such differences will be considered by the judges in the selection
procedures. Any kind of art work done by candidates will be considered,
including classwork, cartoons, homemade toys, maps, etc..

Adapted from forms used by the School Board of Pinellas (FL) County and
Advanced Placement In Studio Art, Educational Testing Service, Princeton,
NJ.

Figure 35. Art portfolio and performance review.

Art Product Evaluation Form

Name of Student	Grade

School	Teacher

Evaluate the student's talent as evidenced in art work on the following scale of 0-5 according to the following criteria. Note that a rating of 5 indicates unique, mature ability and should be used with reservation.

	Not evident	Emerging	Average	Competent	Outstanding	Unique
1. Skillful composition	0	1	2	3	4	5
2. Originality of ideas	0	1	2	3	4	5
3. Complexity and detail	0	1	2	3	4	5
4. Sensitive use of line	0	1	2	3	4	5
5. Sensitive use of color	0	1	2	3	4	5
6. Appropriate use of texture	0	1	2	3	4	5
7. Purposeful use of shape	0	1	2	3	4	5
8. Thoughtful use or space / perspective	0	1	2	3	4	5
9. Effective use of media	0	1	2	3	4	5
10. Expressiveness	0	1	2	3	4	5

Column total   __ __ __ __ __ __

Weight   0   1   2   3   4   5

Weight column total   __ __ __ __ __ __

OVERALL TOTAL   _____

Additional comments: _____

_____

_____

Adapted from: "Evaluation Form for Art Applications", Indianapolis Public
              Schools, School of Performing Arts;
              "Instructions for Scoring the Drawing Test, Form E" Art
              Enrichment: How to Implement a Museum/School Program.
              Austin, TX: The University of Texas at Austin, 1980; and
              "Creative Products Scale - Art", Detroit Public Schools, 1981.

Figure 36. Art product evaluation form.

Biographical Inventory Checklist: Artistically Talented Students

NAME _____   DATE _____

Interviews and biographical sketches will yield self descriptions. Indicators
of the following characteristics tend to be identified with persons with
superior talent.

_____ Very responsible and dependable

_____ enjoys reading literary classics

_____ intends to obtain a college degree

_____ adapts to school rules and regulations

_____ has outstanding sensitivity to the environment

_____ prefers traditional and classical music

_____ is highly competetive

_____ is confident and ambitious

_____ stands up for personal beliefs

_____ feels that school lacks adequate facilities

_____ prefers to work alone

_____ admires artistic teachers

_____ recognizes his/her art abilities

_____ prefers an art career

_____ is willing to alter own art work for improvement

_____ spends a lot of time doing art work

_____ uses imagination in day dreaming, story telling, and art work

_____ is aware that others recognize his/her art talent

Rater Comments:_____   _____
                                                              DATE

_____

Adapted from: Ellison, R., Abe, C., Fox, D., Coray, K., and Taylor, C.
               "Using biographical information in identifying artistic
               talent". in Barbe, W. and Renzulli, J. (Eds).
               Psychology and education of the gifted. New York: Irvington
               Publishers, Inc., 1975 and Wilson, B. and Wilson, M.
               Instruments for the identification of artistic giftedness.
               Paper presented at the NAEA Convention, Chicago, IL., 1981.

Figure 37. Biographical inventory checklist.

APPENDIX C: INSTRUCTIONAL MATERIALS CHECKLISTS

INSTRUCTIONAL MATERIALS CHECKLIST

Title_____   Evaluator_____

Source_____   Date_____

_____   Appropriate Level_____

_____

Cost_____

Content description:_____

_____

_____

_____

Check the appropriate box or boxes in the following:

1. Designed for primary ☐, intermediate ☐, junior high ☐, or high school ☐ levels

2. Designed for student ☐ or teacher ☐ use

3. Designed for individual ☐ or group ☐ use

4. Designed for discovery ☐ or guided ☐ presentation of content

5. Contents present introductory ☐, intermediate ☐, or advanced ☐ concept levels

6. Theme is presented primarily visually ☐ or verbally ☐

7. Presentation is subjective (expressive poetic) ☐ or objective (factual precise) ☐

8. Contents may be used nonsequentially ☐ or have a required sequence ☐

9. Presentation is open-ended (raises questions) ☐ or close-ended (answers questions) ☐

10. Contents planned for consumption by students ☐ or retention by the teacher ☐

Figure 38. Instructional materials checklist.

Resource Evaluation Form

Title_____   Evaluator_____

Source_____   Date_____

_____   Appropriate Level_____

_____

Cost_____

Content Description_____

_____

_____

_____

Check where applicable:	Excellent	Good	Poor
1. Accuracy (objective, timely)			
2. Presentation (parts related, logical)			
3. Applicability (relative to user's level)			
4. Interest (challenging, appealing)			
5. Technical Aspects (clarity of materials)			
6. Practicality (ease of storage, handling, and use; durability)			
Column total			
Weight	3	2	1
Weighted score			

Total Score _____

Recommended for purchase: YES   NO

Adapted from Erickson, C.W.H. (1968). <u>Administering instructional media programs</u>. New York: Macmillan, p. 37.

Figure 39. Resource evaluation form.

APPENDIX D: ADDRESS LIST of RESOURCES

Associations and Organizations

Advanced Placement Program
Studio Art, Drawing, and Art History
Educational Testing Service
Box 977-PD
Princeton, NJ 08541

Alliance for Arts Education
J.F. Kennedy Center for the Performing Arts
2700 F Street, N.W.
Washington, DC 20007

American Association for Gifted Children
15 Gramercy Park
New York, NY 10003

Arts Recognition and Talent Search
300 Northeast 2nd Avenue
Miami, FL 33132

The Association for the Talented and Gifted
Council for Exceptional Children
1920 Association Drive
Reston, VA 22091

Council of Chief State School Officers
1201 16th Street, NW
Washington, DC 20036

Council for Exceptional Children
ERIC Clearinghouse of Handicapped and Gifted Children (CEC/ERIC)
1920 Association Drive
Reston, VA 22091

Creative Education Foundation
State University College at Buffalo
218 Chase Hall
1300 Elmwood Avenue
Buffalo, NY 14222

The Gifted Child Research Institute
300 West 55th Street
New York, NY 10019

MENSA: Gifted Children Program
5304 First Place North
Arlington, VA 22203

National Art Education Association
1916 Association Drive
Reston, VA 22091

National Association for Creative Children and Adults
8080 Spring Valley Drive
Cincinnati, OH 45236

National Association for Gifted Children
5100 North Edgewood Drive
St. Paul, MN 55112

National/State Leadership Training Institute on the Gifted and the Talented
316 West Second Street, Suite Ph-C
Los Angeles, CA 90012

Office of Talented Identification and Development
Johns Hopkins University
Baltimore, MD 21218

Pratt National Talent Search
Pratt Institute
200 Willoughby Avenue
Brooklyn, NY 11205

Rural Education Association
7617 Little River Turnpike, Suite 400
Annandale, VA 22002

World Council for Gifted and Talented Children
Box 218, Teachers College
Columbia University
New York, NY 10027

Journals and Magazines

Arts and Activities
591 Camino de la Reina
Suite 200
San Diego, CA 92108

Art Education
The National Art Education Association
1916 Association Drive
Reston, VA 22091

Challenge: Reaching and Teaching the Gifted Child
Good Apple, Incorporated
Box 299
Carthage, IL 62321-0229

Chart Your Course
G/C/T Publishing Company, Incorporated
Box 6448
Mobile, AL 36660-0448

The Creative Child and Adult Quarterly
The National Association for Creative Children and Adults
8080 Spring Valley Drive
Cincinnati, OH 45236

Exceptional Children
Office for the Journal of The Council for Exceptional Children
1920 Association Drive
Reston, VA 22091

G/C/T
Gifted Creative Talented Children
P.O. Box 66654
Mobile, AL 36606

Gifted Children Newsletter
Gifted and Talented Publications, Incorporated
213 Hollydell Drive
Sewell, NJ 08080

Gifted Child Quarterly
National Association for Gifted Children
5100 North Edgewood Drive
St. Paul, MN 55112

Gifted Education International
AB Academic Publishers
P.O. Box 97
Berkhamsted Herts HP4 2PX ENGLAND

INSEA News
International Society for Education Through Art
Leicester Polytechnic
Scraptoft
Leicester LE7 9SU ENGLAND

Journal of Art and Design Education
33 Cleveland Road
Heaton Moor
Stockport
Chesire SK4 4BS ENGLAND

Journal of Creative Behavior
Creative Education Foundation
State University College at Buffalo
1300 Elmwood Avenue
Buffalo, NY 14222

Journal for Education of the Gifted
University of Denver
School of Education BC 5
Denver, CO 80208

Journal of Multicultural and Crosscultural Research in Art Education
School of Architecture and Allied Arts
Department of Art Education
University of Oregon
Eugene, OR 97403

NAEA NEWS
National Art Education Association
1916 Association Drive
Reston, VA 22091

National/State Leadership Training Institute on the Gifted and Talented Bulletin
N/S LTI/GT
316 West Second Street, Suite PH-C
Los Angeles, CA 90012

North Carolina Association for the Gifted and Talented Quarterly Journal
The North Carolina Association for the Gifted and Talented
Department of Special Education
Applachian State University
Boone, NC 28608

PRISM: A Magazine for the Gifted
PRISM Publishing Company
900 East Broward Blvd.
Fort Lauderdale, FL 33301

Roeper Review
Roeper City and Country School
P.O. Box 329
Bloomfield Hills, MI 48013

School Arts
106 Morningside Drive
Apt. 69A
New York, NY 10027

Studies in Art Education
The National Art Education Association
1916 Association Drive
Reston, VA 22091

USSEA Newsletter
United States Society for Education Through Art
Maryland Institute of Art
705 Bay Street
Baltimore, MD 21211

Visual Arts Research
143 Art and Design Building
4th Street and Peabody Drive
Champaign, IL 61820

BIBLIOGRAPHY

Bachtel-Nash, A. (1984). *National directory: Programs for K–12 artistically gifted and talented students*. Paramount, CA: Tam's Books.

Binet, A., & Simon, Th. (1905). Méthodes nouvelles pour le diagnostic di niveau intellectuel des anormaux. *L'Année psychologique, 11*, 191–244.

Bloom, B.S. (Ed.) (1985). *Developing talent in young people*. New York: Ballantine Books.

Boston, B. O., & Orloff, J. H. (1980). *Preparing to teach the gifted and talented: A guide to personnel development*. Fairfax, VA: Wordsmith.

Clark, G., & Zimmerman, E. (1984). *Educating artistically talented students*. Syracuse, NY: Syracuse University Press.

Cronbach, L. J. (1960). *Essentials of psychological testing* (2nd ed.). New York: Harper and Row.

Eddy, J. (1985). Arts-minded students and their schools of choice. *Network News, 2(1)*, 1–5.

Eisner, E. W. (1967). *The development of drawing characteristics of culturally advantaged and culturally disadvantaged children*. Project No. 3086 (U.S. Department of Health, Education, and Welfare, Office of Education, Bureau of Research).

Ellison, R., Abe, C., Fox, O., Coray, K., & Taylor, C. (1976). Identifying artistic talent. *Gifted Child Quarterly, 20(4)*, 402–13.

Erickson, C. W. H. (1968). *Administering instructional media programs*. New York: Macmillan.

Gallagher, J. J. (1975). *Teaching the gifted child* (2nd ed.). Boston: Allyn and Bacon.

Genetic Studies of Genius:

    Terman, L. M. (1925). *Genetic studies of genius. Vol. 1. Mental and physical traits of a thousand gifted children*. Stanford, CA: Stanford University Press.

    Cox. C. M. (1926). *Genetic studies of genius. Vol. 2. The early mental traits of three thousand geniuses*. Stanford, CA: Stanford University Press.

    Terman, L. M., Burks, B. S., & Jensen, D. W. (1930). *Genetic studies of genius. Vol. 3. The promise of youth: Follow-up studies of a thousand gifted children*. Stanford, CA: Stanford University Press.

Terman, L. M., & Oden, M. (1947). *Genetic studies of genius. Vol. 4. The gifted child grows up: Twenty-five years' follow-up of a superior group*. Stanford, CA: Stanford University Press.

Terman, L. M., & Oden, M. (1959). *Genetic studies of genius. Vol. 5. The gifted child at mid-life: Thirty five years' follow-up of the superior child*. Stanford, CA: Stanford University Press.

Oden, M. (1968). The fulfillment of promise: Forty-year follow-up of the Terman gifted group. *Genetic Psychology Monographs, 77,* 9–93.

Guilford, J. P. (1973). *Creativity tests for children*. Orange, CA: Sheridan Psychological Services.

Graves, M. (1946, 1974, 1978). *Graves design judgment test*. New York: The Psychological Corporation.

Horn, C. C. (1935, 1953). *The Horn art aptitude inventory*. Chicago: C. H. Stoelting.

Jackson, D. M. (1979). The emerging national and state concern. In A. H. Passow. (Ed.). *The gifted and the talented: Their education and development*. Chicago: University of Chicago Press (78th yearbook of NSSE).

Khatena, J. (1981). *Music, art, leadership, and psychomotor abilities assessment records*. Starkville, MS: Allan Associates.

Khatena, J. (1982). *Educational psychology of the gifted*. New York: John Wiley and Sons.

Knauber, A. (1932, 1935). *Knauber art ability test* and *Knauber art vocabulary test*. Published by the author.

Lazarus, E. (1981). *Project art band: A program for visually gifted children*. Lincoln, MA: De Cordova Museum.

Marland, S. P. (1972). *Education of the gifted and talented. Vol. 1. Report to the Congress of the United States by the U.S. Commissioner of Education*. Washington, DC: U.S. Government Printing Office.

Meier, N. C. (1929, 1942, 1963). *Meier art tests*. Iowa City, IA: State University of Iowa, Bureau of Educational Research and Service.

Munro, T., Lark-Horovitz, B., & Barnhardt, E. N. (1942). Children's abilities: Studies at the Cleveland Museum of Art. *Journal of Experimental Education, 11*(2), 97–184.

Newland, T. E. (1976). *The gifted in socioeducational perspective*. Englewood Cliffs, NJ: Prentice Hall.

Pegnato, C. W., & Birch, J. (1959). Locating gifted children in junior high schools: A comparison of methods. *Exceptional Children, 25*(7), 300–304.

P. L. 91–230. (1979). *Elementary and secondary educational amendments of 1969*. Section 806.

Renzulli, J. S., Smith, L. H., White, A. J., Callahan, C. M., & Hartman, R. K. (nd.). *Scales for the rating behavioral characteristics of superior students: Artistic characteristics*. Mansfield Center, CN: Creative Learning Press.

Terman, L. M. (1906). Genius and stupidity: A study of some of the intellectual processes of seven "brighter" and seven "stupid" boys. *Pedagological Seminary, 13,* 307–73.

Thorndike, E. L. (1913). The measurement of achievement in drawing. *Teachers College Record, 14*(5) 345–83.

Witty, P. (1951). *The gifted child*. Boston: D. C. Heath.

Zettel, J. (1979). State provisions for educating the gifted and talented. In A. H. Passow. (Ed.). *The gifted and the talented: Their education and development*. Chicago: University of Chicago Press, (78th Yearbook of NSSE).

RESOURCES FOR EDUCATING ARTISTICALLY TALENTED STUDENTS

was composed in 10-point Mergenthaler Linotron 202 Sabon and leaded 3 points
by Partners Composition;
with display type in Caslon Special initials
provided by Job Litho Services;
printed by sheet-fed offset on 55-pound, acid-free Hi-Brite,
Smyth-sewn and bound over binder's boards in Joanna Arrestox B
by Maple-Vail Book Manufacturing Group, Inc.;
and published by

SYRACUSE UNIVERSITY PRESS
SYRACUSE, NEW YORK 13244-5160